MERRY CHRISTMAS, BABY

ALSO BY DAVE MARSH

Born to Run: The Bruce Springsteen Story

The Rolling Stone Record Guide
    (ed. with John Swenson)

The Book of Rock Lists (with Kevin Stein)

Elvis

Before I Get Old: The Story of the Who

Rocktopicon
    (with Sandra Choron and Debbie Geller)

The First Rock & Roll Confidential Report
    (ed.)

Sun City: The Making of the Record

Trapped: Michael Jackson and the Crossover Dream

Fortunate Son

Glory Days

The Heart of Rock and Soul

50 Ways to Fight Censorship

Pastures of Plenty
    (ed. with Harold Leventhal)

Heaven Is Under Our Feet
    (ed. with Don Henley)

Louie Louie

ALSO BY STEVE PROPES

*Those Oldies but Goodies: A Guide to 50's
    Record Collecting*

Golden Oldies: A Guide to 60's Record Collecting

*Golden Goodies: A Guide to 50's and 60's Popular
    Rock & Roll Record Collecting*

What Was the First Rock and Roll Record?
    (with Jim Dawson)

Merry Christmas, Baby

Holiday Music from Bing to Sting

Dave Marsh
and
Steve Propes

Little, Brown and Company

Boston   New York   Toronto   London

First Edition

Library of Congress Cataloging-in-Publication Data

Marsh, Dave.
    Merry Christmas, baby : holiday music from Bing to Sting /
Marsh and Steve Propes. — 1st ed.
        p.   cm.
    ISBN 0-316-54733-6
    1. Christmas music — History and criticism. 2. Popular music
— History and criticism. I. Propes, Steve. II. Title.
ML3470.M355   1993
782.42'1723 — dc20   93-20372

10 9 8 7 6 5 4 3 2 1

RRD-IN

Designed by Barbara Werden

Published simultaneously in Canada by Little, Brown & Company (Canada) Limited

Printed in the United States of America

To everyone who believes in the spirit of Christmas — may all your Christmases be rockin' and blue

CONTENTS

Merry Christmas, Baby

Introduction

Do You Hear What I Hear?

The Meanings of Christmas Music

*T*HERE MAY HAVE been a time, before the birth of the record industry, when all Christmas music was religious music. But at least since the start of the record age, the musical component of the season has been as much secular as spiritual. A barbershop quartet version of "Jingle Bells" was among the first recordings made in the early days of the century, and pop music has remained a huge part of Christmas record sales ever since some early exec noticed how sales of all music shot up during the holidays. A record (or tape or disc) made a great gift, still does. And a record of a song *about* Christmas . . . what could be more natural?

So artists recorded Christmas classics, reinventing them in their own unique styles. Every kind of music became Christmas music. Hearing "Jingle Bells" in barbershop harmony or as a country waltz, a soul strut, or a big-band powerhouse, listeners found that the novelty alone made the song fresh and put a new sheen on the season. And the records sold, not just in the year of their release, but often for many Christmases thereafter.

Originals fared even better than remakes — think of "White Christmas," "I'll Be Home for Christmas," "Rudolph the Red-Nosed Reindeer" — and so every songwriter and singer turned his or her unique talent to finding a way to celebrate the holiday in music. From Clarence Carter's raunchy soul workout "Back Door Santa" to Darlene Love's heartfelt "Christmas (Baby, Please Come Home)," from Brenda Lee's light-bopping "Rockin' Around the Christmas Tree" to Elmo and Patsy's moronic-but-hilarious "Grandma Got Run Over by a Reindeer," every conceivable emotion found its way at some point into a Christmas tune.

What does it all mean? Chuck Berry, as usual, points us toward an answer. In his autobiography Berry says of his masterpiece, "Sweet Little Sixteen,"

Naturally it was around Christmas when I wrote this one, pumped by

Leonard [Chess] to bring something in for teenagers that could be a Christmas song. . . . Once I started into the Christmas spirit of a kid liking rock 'n' roll, other ideas fell into order.

It's hard to say what's most mind-boggling about this passage: the "naturally," which suggests that anybody asked to knock off a Christmas song for teens could come up with such a joyful paean to youthful exuberance; or the lyrics themselves, which seem to cherish the young girl's innocent greed ("sweet little sixteen / has just got to have . . .") as much as her vitality. In his offhand way, Berry gets to America's heart: our drive to consume defines us as much as any other feature. And this is at no time truer than at Christmas.

As it's practiced today — let's call it Christmas Present — the celebration of Christmas ranks alongside the blues (and its derivatives, from jazz to gospel, from rock and roll to rap), Hollywood movies, the hard-boiled detective novel,

and the streamlined V-8 guzzler, among America's unique contributions to world culture. Christmas Present may be crass and commercial, sentimental and giddy, juvenile and romantic, certainly secular. So is America. We're a young country still, Sweet Little Sixteen at heart. Christmas suits us.

But this American bacchanal of shopping and feasting has loftier sides to it too. It's also a public occasion for expressions of emotion, of commitment to family, of fellow-feeling and love. It's one of the few such occasions in our culture — Valentine's Day and Thanksgiving don't come close. And when these kinds of emotion rise up, only music can meet our needs.

Besides its vitality, it's this emotional component of Christmas music that gives it its greatness, that makes it a subject that rewards contemplation. Reaching down deep, performers have made superb records about longing, nostalgia, love, loneliness, joy, and the myriad other emotions the holiday wrings from us. The emotional heart of

modern Christmas emerges clearly in the four most popular Christmas songs from the mid- and late forties: "White Christmas," "I'll Be Home for Christmas," "The Christmas Song (Chestnuts Roasting on an Open Fire)," and "Merry Christmas, Baby." These songs, all of them adult and quite different from such kiddie fare as the tales of Rudolph, Frosty, and Santa coming to town or landing up on the rooftop, introduce the central themes of our experience of Christmas over the past half century: longing for home, nostalgia for an idealized past, and the potential for conflict between holiday cheer and one's own true inner state.

That's not to suggest that popular Christmas music is without reference to the religious event that inspired it. For us, the pertinent text here is in the gospel from Luke, where it is said that Christ came so "that the thoughts of many hearts may be revealed." It's not blasphemous to suggest that the greatest Christmas music succeeds in just that way, opening our hearts and letting shine all that is within them. What else could motivate a body of work that encompasses Clyde McPhatter and the Drifters' celebratory "White Christmas," Elvis Presley's quavering "Blue Christmas," even Charles Brown's lubricious "Merry Christmas, Baby"? In such transcendent music we find the true meaning of Christmas: to inspire joy in every moment of one's life.

Merry Christmas, Baby was written in the hope of sharing this everyday joy (and as a way of assembling photos of our favorite musicians in Santa hats).

Here's hoping that you enjoy the book, and that your Christmas is white, or blue, or black, or whatever shade you want it to be.

Merry Christmas!

Chapter One

White Christmas

Holiday Music Through the 1940s

AS FAR AS modern Christmas music is concerned, Santa Claus arrived in 1942. That October, *Billboard* magazine, an oversize newssheet for carnival operators and circus barkers that dated back to the turn of the century, initiated a more serious and complete approach to charting record sales. One of its new charts, the Harlem Hit Parade, listed mainly black artists. (Previously, records distributed for the black market were listed alongside country records on a loosely constructed "Folk" chart.) The first Harlem Hit Parade included the Four Ink Spots' "Every Night about This Time," "Cow Cow Boogie" by Freddie Slack with Ella Mae Morse, and "I'm Gonna Move to the Outskirts of Town" by Louis Jordan.

The third Harlem Hit Parade, in the *Billboard* of November 5, 1942, featured a new entry at position number seven.

The record had been issued by Decca, the home label for many of the most important black artists of the day, including the very popular Ink Spots and Jordan, the most popular black artist of the decade. But a white artist made this record: It was Bing Crosby's "White Christmas." And its appeal to Americans transcended all categories, including the difficult-to-breach barriers of race.

On the pop charts, "White Christmas" had already appeared for a full month; it would spend a total of seventeen weeks there, eleven of them at number one. For the recording industry, Christmas as we know it had begun.

Irving Berlin wrote "White Christmas" for a movie called *Holiday Inn* (1942), an implausible tale of an inn that opened only on holidays. While the composer grew heated in the writing, and Bing Crosby immediately loved it, others were dubious. After the first New York screening, Berlin's staff returned to the office convinced that the boss's big number had flopped.

Ten Top-Selling Christmas Singles

1. Bing Crosby, "White Christmas" (1942)

2. The Harry Simeone Chorale, "The Little Drummer Boy" (1958)

3. Bobby Helms, "Jingle Bell Rock" (1957)

4. Charles Brown, "Please Come Home for Christmas" (1961)

5. Nat "King" Cole, "The Christmas Song" (1946)

6. Elvis Presley, "Blue Christmas" (1964)

7. Brenda Lee, "Rockin' Around the Christmas Tree" (1958)

8. Clyde McPhatter and the Drifters, "White Christmas" (1954)

9. Earl Grant, "Silver Bells" (1966)

10. The Chipmunks with David Seville, "The Chipmunk Song" (1958)

Source: *Billboard* magazine

What saved "White Christmas" were requests made by GIs to Armed Forces Radio around the world. Soldiers away from home, many of them in the South Pacific or North Africa, uncertain of whether they'd ever again see family and friends, let alone a snowfall, responded passionately to Berlin's understated evocation of the mythic romance of Christmas Past. ("Keep it simple! Keep it simple!" he'd continually insisted to the amanuensis who helped him write it down.)

The song's slow start in America, Berlin eventually decided, was because of the opening verse about Christmas in a warm California clime. He ordered the first verse cut from the sheet music (to resounding initial complaints from music stores, who felt they were being cheated of material), and Bing Crosby's hit record climbed the charts without it. About the only place you can hear anything but the chorus today is on the version Darlene Love sang in 1963 on Phil Spector's *A Christmas Gift for You from Phil Spector.* In the ensuing ten years, "White Christmas" sold three million copies as sheet music, while Crosby's rendition sold more than nine million records. Other artists sold another five million of the same song. It was for many years — and perhaps remains today — the largest-selling single song, Christmas-related or otherwise, ever waxed.

"White Christmas" changed Christmas music forever, both by revealing the huge potential market for Christmas songs and by establishing the themes of home and nostalgia that would run through Christmas music evermore. But it hardly stands as the first Christmas hit. Tin Pan Alley had been turning out commercial Christmas-related songs for many years, at least as far back as "Jingle Bells" in the mid-nineteenth century, and the advent of recording almost immediately spawned Christmas hits.

The very earliest known Christmas recordings came from the Hayden Quartet, a barbershop-style harmony group. "Jingle Bells" hit for them in 1902, followed by "Silent

Night, Hallowed Night" in 1905. The Columbia Mixed Quartet, another barbershop quartet, scored with "Hark! The Herald Angels Sing" in 1916, followed by the Peerless Quartet, also on Columbia, with "Christmas Time at Pumpkin Center" in 1919. The Peerless group also hit with "Auld Lang Syne" in 1921.

In 1928, Paul Whiteman remade "Silent Night," featuring a sensational young vocalist named Bing Crosby. One reason Der Bingle responded with such assurance to "White Christmas" may have been his successful experience with Yuletide tunes; he'd already sold several million copies of his solo version of "Silent Night," backed with "Adeste Fideles," in 1935.

In 1934, black jazz band leader Clarence Williams introduced the jive-talking "Christmas Night in Harlem." That same year produced an early version of "Winter Wonderland" by the Freddy Martin Orchestra — a release that proved so successful that

the better-known Ted Weems immediately covered it — and the original recording of "Santa Claus Is Coming to Town," by George Hall and His Orchestra, a Bluebird label "sweet" (that is, corny) band. "Santa Claus" went on to become the third-best-selling Christmas tune of all time, but it had already spent two years on the shelf while writers Haven Gillespie and J. Fred Coots tried to find someone to perform it. Eddie Cantor employed Coots as a staff writer but even he wouldn't go near the thing until his wife, Ida, persuaded him to give it one chance, on his radio program a week before Thanksgiving in 1934. Crosby, this time in conjunction with the Andrews Sisters, and Perry Como both sold millions of copies of the song in later years.

In 1935, alongside Crosby's solo effort, Benny Goodman recorded a jazzed-up "Jingle Bells." In 1936, two of America's most original talents came to the Christmas party when Fats Waller recorded "Swingin' the Jingle Bells," matched with Louis Prima's jivey "What Will Santa Claus Say?" Neither sold very well. Prewar America still insisted on taking Christmas straight.

The 1930s ended with the square, the hip, the outrageous. The square was "'Twas the Night Before Christmas," Milton Cross's musical setting of "A Visit from St. Nicholas," the Clement Moore verse tale that replaced the gaunt European St. Nicholas with the jolly, corpulent American concept of Santa Claus. The hip included "Gin for Christmas" by soon-to-be-venerable jazz vibes player Lionel Hampton, "The Man with the Whiskers" by the Hoosier Hot Shots, a hillbilly (this was before the more delicate term *country* was invented) combo from the "National Barn Dance" radio show, and "Hello, Mr. Kringle" by the Kay Kyser Orchestra, one of the hotter white swing bands.

The outrageous was Ben Light and his Surf Club Boys, whose "Christmas Balls" burned with as many double entendres as your average pine tree has branches. According to the disc jockey Dr. Demento, Light's song was such a favorite upon release that it attracted the attention of primitive record bootleggers even in the 1940s. Despite the disapprobation of contemporary Tipper Gores, many unauthorized copies surfaced during the decade, until Larry Vincent spun off a less scandalous remake called "Xmas Tree Song" in about 1946. "Christmas Balls" kicked off one of the hidden trends in Christmas music, the novelty song that expresses — always humorously — doubts about the ultimate import of seasonal good cheer. In this respect, Light and "Balls" are the progenitors of every Christmas travesty from "All I Want for Christmas (Is My Two Front Teeth)" to "Grandma Got Run Over by a Reindeer."

With the world at the brink of war, the pace stepped up. The 1940s began with Sammy Kaye's "Santa Claus Is on His Way" in 1941, which used a lyric with a topical reference to Walter

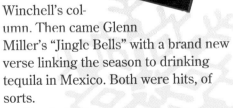

Winchell's column. Then came Glenn Miller's "Jingle Bells" with a brand new verse linking the season to drinking tequila in Mexico. Both were hits, of sorts.

Also in 1941 came the first known Christmas blues, recorded most appropriately by Leadbelly, whose "Christmas Song" was released on the tiny Asch label (predecessor to proprietor Moe Asch's more famous Folkways). Born Huddie Ledbetter in 1888, this powerful black folk-blues creator spent many of his years locked up in Angola Prison in Louisiana, the very place he was discovered during a 1933 field recordings trip. In "Christmas Song," Leadbelly added a contemporary touch of cynicism to the Yule music mix, taking a young fellow to the top of the tallest hill in his neighborhood to look far out over the valley and see "if Christmas really is coming."

There were at least two 1942 covers of "White Christmas," by the orchestras of Freddy Martin and of Gordon Jenkins. Bing Crosby himself released three additional Christmas titles in 1942: "Adeste Fidelis" and "Silent Night" (reissues of his 1935 titles), plus "God Rest Ye Merry, Gentlemen." Roy Rogers recorded a cowboy version of "Silent Night," the first example of country Christmas vocalizing, for Decca's folk series, while Fred Waring (who later invented the blender of the same name) remade "'Twas the Night Before Christmas," fronting his Pennsylvanians.

"White Christmas" kept returning to the top ten in 1943 and 1944, the year that Frank Sinatra's version appeared. If "White Christmas" had established a new seasonal theme — the longing for the comforts of home and the way things used to be (whether or not they'd ever actually been quite so pacific and pastoral as memory claimed — the first to pick up on it was again Crosby. His "I'll Be Home for Christmas," a wartime promise disguised as a holiday greeting (something in the manner of the English hit "White Cliffs of Dover") climbed all the way to number three in 1943. Also in 1944, Judy Garland recorded the original version of "Have Yourself a Merry Little Christmas," a song later associated with Sinatra.

In 1945, World War II ended, but not the seasonal nostalgia it had unleashed. More important, popular music was about to give way to new forms, new ideas, new sounds, new artists. Crosby's original "White Christmas" reached number one again, a feat it would repeat in 1947, the year Berlin's biggest number was also covered by the Ink Spots. But in 1946, "White Christmas" didn't chart at all. That intervening year belonged to the King Cole Trio.

The King Cole Trio, both an instrumental and a vocal unit, can be traced back to the late 1930s. It featured pianist

Dave Marsh's Twelve Hits of Christmas

1. Darlene Love,
"Christmas (Baby Please Come Home)"

2. Clyde McPhatter and the Drifters,
"White Christmas"

3. Otis Redding, "Merry Christmas, Baby"

4. Marion Williams and the Stars of Faith,
"Hallelujah"

5. Bing Crosby, "Do You Hear What I Hear?"

6. Bruce Springsteen,
"Santa Claus Is Coming to Town"

7. Stevie Nicks, "Silent Night"

8. Stevie Wonder, "One Little Christmas Tree"

9. Charles Brown,
"Please Come Home for Christmas"

10. Bob and Doug McKenzie,
"Twelve Days of Christmas"

11. James Brown, "Let's Make This Christmas
Mean Something This Year"

12. The Orioles,
"What Are You Doing New Year's Eve"

Special Three-Song Bonus EP

1. Donny Hathaway, "This Christmas"

2. Aretha Franklin, "Winter Wonderland"

3. Gayla Peevey, "I Want a Hippopotamus for Christmas"

and lead singer Nat "King" Cole, guitarist Oscar Moore, and bassist Wesley Prince (who was later replaced by Johnny Miller). Their first hit, "Straighten Up and Fly Right" in 1944, firmly established the fledgling Capitol label. Leader Cole recorded two versions of "The Christmas Song" in August of 1946. One, the simpler trio recording, was not immediately issued. An alternate take, sweetened with strings, was released, and it charted at number three. Though this original version did well, it was kept on the market for only one or two years at most. By 1948, Cole had decided to abandon the smaller trio sound in favor of the more commercial pop vocal.

Written by the then little-known singer Mel Torme and Robert Wells, "The Christmas Song" is suffused in the same fuzzily reminiscent glow — best expressed in its subtitle, "Chestnuts Roasting on an Open Fire" — as "White Christmas," and its impact was just as immediate. In 1947 "The Christmas Song" was covered by Bing Crosby, in

1949 it was remade by Les Brown, and in 1951 by Patti Page.

Postwar popular music differed from the Tin Pan Alley and Broadway sensibilities that dominated it for the previous century largely because it opened up to voices from a much more diverse selection of Americans — and these voices gradually began to be heard by *all* pop music audiences, not just a select few who sought "authenticity." Rather than Stephen Foster, Irving Berlin, or George Gershwin interpreting black rhythms and experiences, African-American singers and musicians themselves appeared in the charts. Rather than Rodgers and Hammerstein's "Oklahoma!" hokum, real country singers had a chance to hit the charts. The change occurred gradually and not without controversy. But the general trend proved irreversible.

Christmas music was almost immediately affected, not only by the appearance of relatively smooth-toned, black-skinned stylists like the King Cole Trio and the Ink Spots, but by the appearance of the first cowboy Christmas songs. One of the earliest country Christmas records was "Empty Chairs at the Christmas Table," by longtime roadhouse maestro Bob Wills and his Texas Playboys. Another, "Christmas Carols by the Old Corral," came from newcomer Tex Ritter. Neither of these scenes would have been likely in the previous "over the hills and through the woods to grandmother's house we go" popular music culture. Not that that sensibility had entirely disappeared: Vaughn Monroe had considerable 1945 success with the Sammy Cahn/Jule Styne sing-a-long "Let It Snow! Let It Snow! Let It Snow!" Their snowbound scenario — which never mentions Christmas — enjoyed further success with a 1950 remake by Frank Sinatra.

More Christmas blues also appeared on the 1946 charts, in Champion Jack Dupree's "Santa Claus Blues" and something by Gatemouth Moore called "Christmas Blues," a title that would be used for several different songs later in the decade.

In 1947 another song with that name enabled a King Cole Trio–inspired combo to come forth with the earliest rhythm-and-blues Christmas classic. "Merry Christmas, Baby" was credited to Johnny Moore's Three Blazers. Moore led the trio and he came by his Cole influence honestly, for Oscar Moore, Cole's guitarist, was his brother. But it was the Charles Brown vocal that sold the song. And, at least in his own account, it was also Charles Brown who put it together:

A guy named Lou Baxter used to follow us around; he had a little satchel. He said, "Charles Brown, tell you what. I got a song I want you to do."
"What is it?"
"Just look through my satchel. You'll find it."
I looked in there and saw "Merry Christmas Blues," which was not "Merry Christmas Baby." I said, "That looks good." It gave me an idea, so I wrote the words to that. Lou wanted to get $500 so every time

you record anybody's number, advance them $500. I fixed it up, did it, put Lou Baxter's name on it. My name was supposed to go on it. We went on the road. They [presumably the record company owners] put Johnny Moore's name on it.

Whoever composed it, whoever got the credit, the genius of "Merry Christmas, Baby" came from putting the right holiday with the right music, in that Brown's smooth vocal stylings blended easily into the school of Nat Cole emulators, only deeper. It also linked a holiday with an urge, a pretty girl, a kiss, or "a few," something slightly intoxicating to ingest. It portrayed the adult Christmas and did so from the heart of the blues. Cool, and with its lyric literally dripping with Christmas and other holiday baubles, "Merry Christmas, Baby" took the most somber look at the season of joy yet, making "I'll Be Home for Christmas" seem awash in optimism.

The black-owned, Los Angeles–based Exclusive Records released

STEVE PROPES'S CHRISTMAS BAKER'S DOZEN

1. Johnny Moore's Three Blazers, "Merry Christmas, Baby"
2. Clyde McPhatter and the Drifters, "White Christmas"
3. The Youngsters, "Christmas in Jail"
4. Brenda Lee, "Rockin' Around the Christmas Tree"
5. Huey "Piano" Smith and the Clowns, "Silent Night"
(or anything else from their LP 'Twas the Night Before Christmas)
6. The Moonglows, "Hey Santa Claus"
7. Bobby Helms, "Jingle Bell Rock"
8. The Salas Brothers, "Donde Esta Santa Claus"
9. Mabel Scott, "Boogie Woogie Santa Claus"
10. The Shells, "Happy Holiday"
11. Chuck Berry, "Run Rudolph Run"
12. Charles Brown, "Please Come Home for Christmas"
13. Darlene Love, "Christmas (Baby Please Come Home)"

"Merry Christmas, Baby" in December of 1947. It hit a respectable but not spectacular number three on the Race Records chart (which had replaced the Harlem Hit Parade in early 1945). But, as with both Crosby's and Cole's impressive evergreens, "Merry Christmas, Baby" became a chart perennial, hitting the Race charts in both 1948 and 1949 and staying in print on one label or another to this day.

In 1956, Charles Brown re-recorded "Merry Christmas, Baby" for Aladdin, the label for which he toiled long after the Johnny Moore trio split up. Since then it has been recorded often, by all sorts of singers, most notably by Otis Redding and, in an arrangement identical to Redding's, Bruce Springsteen.

In 1947 Gene Autry came up with a new favorite, the child-pleasing "Here Comes Santa Claus." Written by Autry with Oakey Haldeman, it began a linkage with the holiday spirit that Autry would claim for decades, though not primarily because of "Here Comes Santa Claus." The first significant country cousin cover of this classic was by Red Foley in 1949, followed by remakes by Jimmy Boyd in 1953 and Sheb Wooley in 1958.

Sarah Vaughan gave "The Lord's Prayer" a Christmas feeling in 1947 and inspired similar recordings in 1949 by Perry Como; by two of the most important black vocal groups, the Ink Spots and the Orioles, in 1950; throughout the fifties, by various female artists, including Mahalia Jackson and Marie Knight (both in 1951), Dinah Washington (1953), and Jackson again in 1956; and in the seventies by Barbra Streisand.

The Ink Spots became a popular-music institution in 1939 with the phenomenal success of their "If I Didn't Care." They were the most important black vocal group in America, thanks to their willingness to superserve the pop market with a distinctive blend of agreeable and self-deprecating harmonies. In that spirit, Decca had them remake "White Christmas." It didn't chart, though — not on the race charts, not on the pop charts. But a major surprise awaited. A funkier, more street-smart black singing group, the Ravens, not only put a rhythm-and-blues definition to their remake of "White Christmas," they also took it to the streets and to the charts — at least the race charts. The differing success of the two versions suggests the changes taking place in the music industry as a whole, for the very ethnic music identity that the Ink Spots had been forced to downplay, the Ravens stepped forward to emphasize.

As with the Ink Spots, the Ravens' flip side was "Silent Night," with which the group first charted in late 1948. Their "White Christmas" showed up on the charts in the first *Billboard* of 1949. A style shift had passed between generations of pop music through the Ravens' unique combination of bass lead Jimmy Ricks and the sweeping tenor Maite Marshall. "Silent Night" returned in 1949 via a gospel treatment given it by Sister Rosetta Tharpe, a version remade by Mahalia Jackson in 1950.

The fate of pop music now fell into the hands of rhythm and blues. The R&B vocal style that became popularly known as doowop was being created by various vocal groups of the late 1940s. The earliest of the new groups to record was the Ravens in 1947, but the most

revolutionary was the Baltimore-based Orioles, led by Sonny Til, who first recorded "It's Too Soon to Know" in 1948.

Though the Orioles and Ravens were contemporaries, and both sounded overtly "blacker" than the Ink Spots, their styles were antithetical. Cool and suave to the Ravens' bold and swinging, the Orioles came up with the first great *original* seasonal R&B-group classic with their 1948 ballad "(It's Gonna Be a) Lonely Christmas." Although in its first year of release it charted no better and no worse than the Ravens, the song was reissued with greater success in late 1949, when it was mated to a new flip side, "What Are You Doing New Year's Eve." Featuring a creamy Til lead against a softly humming vocal background and simple piano and organ notes, by the time Sonny pops that "jackpot question in advance" the second time, the Orioles have created a harmony masterpiece that transcends its season.

The combination of "Lonely Christmas" and "What Are You Doing New Year's Eve" made up one of the best rhythm-and-blues double ballads ever waxed, and served as one of the primary models for the burgeoning doowop style. With the Ravens countering with "Silent Night" backed with Jimmy Ricks's rocking bass lead "White Christmas," and two other black-group versions of "White Christmas" also appearing — by the Sentimentalists in late 1948 and by the Highlanders during late 1949 — the age of the rhythm-and-blues Christmas had arrived.

Mabel Scott, at one time married to Charles Brown, ended 1948 with her brilliant "Boogie Woogie Santa Claus," which was remade by Patti Page for Christmas of 1950. Scott's record also pioneered the practice of giving the boogie treatment to Christmas standards. Most important, veteran vocalist Big Joe Turner, one of the original boogie-woogie performers of the late thirties, cut "Christmas Date Boogie" in 1948.

To the trade, the year 1949 was of major technological significance. It was the year that two major labels began the war of the configurations. The first shot was fired by RCA Victor, which in early 1949 introduced the seven-inch 45-rpm record, followed in turn by Columbia, which premiered the twelve-inch, 33⅓-rpm "microgroove" long-playing album, or LP. RCA won the battle — for the next couple of decades, the most important barometer of record success would continue to be the single song on seven inches of wax or plastic — but lost the war as albums proved more desirable and thus more profitable.

Prior to 1949, albums were essentially record books, containing a half dozen or so individual 78-rpm records, which together made up the theme of the work. Various Christmas works were issued in this form, including albums by Sinatra, Crosby, and Como. The LP changed all that. At first, these LPs were ten inches in diameter, but within a year or so, twelve inches emerged as the industry standard.

Another marketing innovation directly connected to Christmas records emerged in the late forties with Gene Autry's "Here Comes Santa Claus" and "Rudolph the Red-Nosed Reindeer." Those discs came with the earliest examples of the 45-rpm picture sleeve. This was little more than a sales technique based on the theory that if a youngster or his mother were shopping for records, and the kid spotted a colorful cartoon picture of Santa on the sleeve of "Here Comes Santa Claus," junior would pester mom until she put some cash into the pocket of the shrewd record marketer. Picture sleeves soon became a prestige part of any single release, and remained so until the 45 bit the dust in the digital era.

Such devices proved especially crucial because the record industry of the forties was totally centered on Christmas; as much as a third of all sales, and perhaps an even higher percentage of profits, came in the six weeks between Thanksgiving and the first of the year. Superstar new releases — not necessarily holiday-oriented, but just *product* — were practically demanded. This remained the case through the sixties, when Capitol would periodically cannibalize "excess" tracks from English Beatles albums to ensure a holiday release from their Liverpudlian cash

Dr. Demento's Demented Christmas Favorites

1. Elmo and Patsy,
"Grandma Got Run Over by a Reindeer"

2. Weird Al Yankovic,
"Christmas at Ground Zero"

3. Spike Jones, "All I Want for Christmas
(Is My Two Front Teeth)"

4. Stan Freberg, "Green Christma$"

5. Stan Freberg and Daws Butler,
"Christmas Dragnet"

6. Tom Lehrer, "Christmas Carol"
(from An Evening Wasted with Tom Lehrer)

7. The Chipmunks, "The Chipmunk Song"

8. The Waitresses, "Christmas Wrapping"

9. Yogi Yorgesson,
"I Yust Go Nuts at Christmas"

10. The Bob Rivers Comedy Corp,
"Twelve Pains of Christmas"
(from Twisted Christmas)

(Dr. Demento, also known as record collector Barry Hansen,
hosts one of syndicated radio's most popular programs. He has also heard
virtually every Christmas record known to man.)

cows, and well into the seventies, when contemporary marketing techniques finally liberated the record biz from Santa's shadow.

Though abundant new technologies eventually paved the way for that everyday prosperity, in the late forties, changing standards and the inability of the industry to settle on the size and speed of their releases produced competitive chaos, in which two of the three biggest labels — Decca, the third, was a bystander — couldn't agree on anything. The earliest label to incorporate all three speeds (33⅓, 45, and 78) was the emergent major, Capitol (significantly, the first important pop label to base itself in California, away from the usual corporate folderol). The original Christmas long-play album was a Capitol country disc, Jimmy Wakely's *Christmas on the Range,* released in late 1949. It was the third LP Capitol issued.

New Christmas pop standards were thinner than snowfall in April during those late forties years. Only one emerged in 1948, Frank Sinatra's original of "Have Yourself a Merry Little Christmas," an oft-redone smoothie the Chairman himself was to record again in 1963 for his own Reprise label.

Sinatra recorded at Columbia, which had invented the LP. But Sinatra's 1948 Christmas album, *Christmas Songs by*

Sinatra, was released in 78 form that year, and not on LP until late 1949 (as the sixteenth LP on the label). The album would be retitled *Christmas with Sinatra* in 1954, then *Christmas Dreaming* in 1957, and *Have Yourself a Merry Little Christmas* in 1966. It is now once more known as *Christmas Dreaming,* on compact disc. These four title changes are likely an all-time high for repackaging, even in a business noted for constant repackaging and reissuing.

The other important trendsetters of the late forties were musical, not technical: novelty gagsters and singing cowboys. Cowboys were steady sources for 1948 seasonal interpretations, with vocalist Cowboy Copas offering his country take on "White Christmas" for the pioneer Cincinnati indie King Records, a version sufficiently popular for King to reissue it in 1951. For Capitol, Jimmy Wakely recorded "Christmas on the Range" and Tex Ritter did "Merry Christmas Polka," which was covered by Wakely in 1949.

Gene Autry followed "Here Comes Santa Claus" with his much more acclaimed "Rudolph the Red-Nosed Reindeer" in 1949. Autry's "Rudolph" became the second-best-selling Christmas hit up till then, but not without a struggle much more difficult than Berlin's with "White Christmas."

"Rudolph" represents another landmark in the complete secularization of Christmas as a marketing vehicle, for he was born to the Montgomery Ward stores as a promotion

gimmick. In 1939, and for several years thereafter, Ward's gave this poem, written by advertising copywriter Robert L. May, as a gift to shoppers. As World War II loomed, then dawned, the story of Rudolph, the red-nosed savior of Santa's nearly aborted Christmas Eve journey, resonated with special force. But by 1947, Ward's no longer needed the critter, and its owners made an outright gift of the copyright to May. May found a book publisher for the story and sold a hundred thousand copies the first year. In 1949 May and his brother-in-law, veteran composer Johnny Marks, came up with the jingle-like tune that accompanied the verse. They took the song first to Perry Como, one of the biggest pop stars of the day, but Como wouldn't sing it unless they changed a line, and May wasn't about to mess with a gold mine. So they approached Gene Autry.

"The song came to me because I had a hit with Columbia with 'Here Comes Santa Claus' and it was a million seller," Autry said.

"I was looking for another hit, so a New York songwriter, Johnny Marks, sent me an acetate demo of 'Rudolph.' I wasn't going to record it, but my wife liked it — it reminded her of the 'Ugly Duckling' — so I decided to record it, thinking it wouldn't be a hit. Of course, it was, the biggest hit Columbia had until then. I think it's sold close to ten million by now." It sold its first two million right away, in 1949, and charted regularly for several years thereafter.

In addition to the Autry version's reappearance, "Rudolph" was covered at least five times in 1950: by country star Red Foley, who had already covered Autry's "Here Comes Santa Claus"; by pop singers Bing Crosby and Primo Scala; by Sugar Chile Robinson, a black boogie-woogie child prodigy from Detroit; and by Spike Jones. Jones's "Rudolph the Red-Nosed Reindeer" was more of a parody of a novelty than a cover, proving, it may be, that there's danger in mocking children's heroes, although Spike had already established — as we shall see — that mocking

A Western Swing Christmas with Bob Wills' Original Texas Playboys

children was more than acceptable.

In 1953, country comics Homer and Jethro, who spoofed everything from "How Much Is That Doggie in the Window?" to "Hound Dog" (in fact, another of their 1953 satires was "How Much Is That Hound Dog in the Window?," a satire on Big Mama Thornton's "Hound Dog" three years before Elvis's hit with his cover version,

which Homer and Jethro also parodied), came up with their own take on "Rudolph." So did wunderkind Jimmy Boyd, with "Reindeer Rock," in 1955. Doowop's Cadillacs waited until 1956 to do theirs. "Run Rudolph Run" by Chuck Berry in 1959 brought the character, if not the song, fully to the rock-and-roll era. By the mid-eighties, more than three hundred records about Rudolph had been made — more than any song this side of "White Christmas," "Louie, Louie," or "Yesterday" — and the publishers claimed more than ninety million copies sold. Rudolph has had his own TV special, and that bright red nose is as familiar to today's kids as Santa's cheery cherry cheeks.

Cowboys controlled Christmas caroling in 1949. In addition to Autry, there were offerings like Bob Wills and the Texas Playboys' "Santa Is on His Way"; Eddy Arnold's double-sided "Will Santa Come to Shanty Town?" and "C-H-R-I-S-T-M-A-S" (an early example of an innovative 45-rpm release issued in conjunction with the regular 78-rpm record in 1949, about six months after the 45 was introduced early that year); and Roy Rogers and Dale Evans's "Christmas on the Plains," an adaptation of Wakely's earlier "Christmas on the Range." Lost in the first great Year of Rudolph was a gentle Ernest Tubb country ballad, an offbeat take on "White Christmas" that would reach out as one of the holiday's greatest efforts, his original "Blue Christmas." (Almost a decade later, Elvis Presley would revive the song with a now classic reading.) That same year, Tubb also gave a country feel to "White Christmas."

Just as pervasive through the late forties were the novelty gagsters. Working in the great tradition established by Ben Light's "Christmas Balls," Spike Jones scored the first blow with "All I Want for Christmas (Is My Two Front Teeth)," which reached the charts in 1948. The song is far more sardonic than most listeners, caught up in its cuteness, have ever appreciated, but in any event, once Spike and his City Slickers cut loose on it the results were immediate and predictable: crash, bam, to the toppermost of the poppermost. Both the Andrews Sisters and Danny Kaye attempted to compete directly with Jones in 1949, but they failed to dent the popularity of the original twisted take, and Spike's place amongst the most hallowed Christmas hitsters remains secure.

Jones's sibilant success proved a mere harbinger of a landslide of novelties that would appear in the fifties. Also ahead of the trend was popular ethnic comedian Yogi Yorgesson (real name Harry Stewart). His "Yingle Bells" backed with "I Yust Go Nuts at Christmas," a 1949 double-sided original that was reissued in 1957, continues as a popular novelty standard.

The music of Christmas Present was now established. Some of the most important songs of the era had been written and given definitive versions; styles had been fixed from which future Yule hitmakers would wring their changes. Throughout the years to come, "White Christmas" and its brethren continued to speak to us. In the fifties, however, they were about to pick up the same kind of new accents as the rest of popular music.

Chapter Two

I Saw Mommy Kissing Santa Claus

The Triumph of Novelty

THE KEY SONGS of modern Christmas music, notably "White Christmas," "Rudolph the Red-Nosed Reindeer," and "Merry Christmas, Baby," sprang up in the forties. But the fifties undoubtedly produced the greatest number of enduring Christmas records. That's not surprising, given the decade's popular music crazy quilt, in which rhythm and blues, rock and roll, country and western, jazz, and an unending stream of novelties joined the mainstream of American pop.

In the first year of the decade, Decca finally released the label's earliest Christmas album (Decca's eighteenth LP). The artist was none other than Bing Crosby, the title was none other than *White Christmas*, and this 1950 effort stayed in the Decca (later MCA) catalog well into the 1970s. Decca actually released three holiday LPs by Crosby in 1950: after *White Christmas* came *Christmas Greetings*, which was followed by *A Christmas Story, the Small One*.

Gene Autry's Christmas of 1950 promised to be as lucrative as his final several from the forties when he came up with "Frosty the Snow Man," a major hit for him even though it was quickly covered by Red Foley, Roy Rogers, Nat "King" Cole, and Jimmy Durante. In 1953, two additional versions of "Frosty the Snow Man" surfaced, by Jimmy Boyd and Hank Snow.

Like Rudolph, Frosty (created by songwriters Steve Nelson and

Jack Rollins, whose catalog is otherwise unprepossessing) immediately became an important new character in the mid-winter festivities. More fairy-tale-like than "Rudolph," "Frosty" recounted the short but brilliant life of the world's most animated snow man. From the fifties through today, depictions of Frosty have frequently turned up on Christmas merchandise, always wearing that magical silk hat, and carrying his corncob pipe just beneath his button nose. By 1969 *Frosty the Snow Man* had become a TV special, with its own soundtrack album; the special still is rerun every year, though the soundtrack has long since faded into obscurity.

Nashville in 1950 also turned out a country swing variation on a classic, Johnny Bond's "Jingle Bells Boogie." It serves as a thematic ancestor of Bobby Helms's 1957 hit, "Jingle Bell Rock."

Blues fans had three Christmas choices in 1950: New Orleans crooner

Larry Darnell's "It's Gonna Be a Blue Christmas," Lowell Fulson's major hit "Lonesome Christmas," which has been reissued for decades, and Johnny Otis's "Far Away Christmas Blues," with a vocal featuring Little Esther. Jazz buyers dug Ella Fitzgerald's risqué cleverness in "Santa Claus Got Stuck in My Chimney," a song so salacious that her man-agement currently refuses to allow this fine Yule tidbit be reissued.

Christmas 1951 brought four consecutive Mercury releases from Patti Page: the reissue of her "Boogie Woogie Santa Claus," originally issued in 1950, and new renditions of "Jingle Bells," "Santa Claus Is Coming to Town," and "The Christmas Song." The flip side of Page's "Boogie Woogie Santa Claus" was a remake of a minor hit by Pee Wee King from 1948. After a few weeks, it became evident that this flip, a countri-fied weeper called "Tennessee Waltz," was the hit side, but soon it was much more than that. "Tennessee Waltz" sold into the millions, making it the biggest hit of the pre–rock-and-roll 1950s. By early 1951, Page's "Tennessee Waltz" had been hooked up with a new nonholiday flip side. Later that year, Mercury Records tried once again with Page's "Boogie Woogie Santa Claus," along with her earliest holiday LP, *Christmas with Patti Page*. Reissued on the company's budget label in 1955, the LP stayed

Ten Best Christmas Novelty Records

1. Babs Gonzales, "Be Bop Santa Claus"
(Proving, among other things, that rap records well predate the 1980s.)

2. The Salas Brothers, "Donde Esta Santa Claus"
(The original of this Spanish-language kiddie plea was done by Augie Rios in 1958, but the best was this 1966 East LA remake by young Rudy and Steve Salas.)

3. Spike Jones, "All I Want for Christmas (Is My Two Front Teeth)"
(That lisp is the gimmick of all time.)

4. Stan Freberg, "Christmas Dragnet," aka "Yulnet"
(Any record that pisses off Jack Webb has to be great.)

5. Buchanan and Goodman, "Santa and the Satellite"
(Possibly their best record of all time — certainly better than their big hit, "Flying Saucer.")

6. Little Lambsie Penn, "I Want to Spend Christmas with Elvis"
(It's hard not to like this Atco label release, especially since the songwriter was Bobby Darin, one year before Atco got smart, dumped Lambsie, and added Darin to its roster.)

7. Eddy Lawrence, "The Old Philosopher"
(Yes, that's what's botherin' me . . .)

8. Gayla Peevey, "I Want a Hippopotamus for Christmas"
(Tops the Most Ridiculous list.)

9. Bob and Doug McKenzie, "Twelve Days of Christmas"
(For beer drinkers only.)

10. Lalo Guerrero, "Pancho Claus"
(East LA's Stan Freberg takes on Feliz Navidad.)

in print until the 1970s. Also checking in with "Jingle Bells" was multitrack pioneer and guitarist's guitarist Les Paul, whose arrangement was the predecessor of Chet Atkins's 1955 instrumental version.

In 1951 Columbia finally got around to issuing Gene Autry's first Christmas LP, *Merry Christmas with Gene Autry* (retitled *Rudolph the Red-Nosed Reindeer* in 1964), while *Perry Como Sings Merry Christmas Music* was the kickoff RCA Victor Christmas LP. Both of these were pastiche releases of earlier 78-rpm booklet-style albums, rather than new recordings. The market for albums of original, versus recycled, Christmas recordings hadn't yet been established to the major labels' satisfaction.

Kay Starr's pop-jazz contribution to the 1951 holiday was "The Man with the Bag." But more typical of the era's straight pop selections was a release by children's media favorite Howdy Doody, who brought forth "Howdy Doody and Santa Claus." The year produced no rhythm-and-blues classics, even though Louis Jordan, the most popular black recording star of the 1940s, finally got around to putting his stamp on Christmas with "May Every Day Be Christmas." But his star had peaked.

Diligent Jordan disciple Bill Haley did come up with his countrified "A Year Ago This Christmas" in 1951, but it was three years before Haley's landmark hit,

"Rock Around the Clock," and the disc made no noise. Classic black vocal groups had Christmas releases, great songs — everything but hits. The Five Keys, a group from Newport News, Virginia, that had a hit with "Glory of Love" in 1951, finished the year with "It's Christmastime," while the Robins briefly became the Nic Nacs and recorded "Gonna Have a Merry Christmas" with Mickey Champion, a duplicate of "Double Crossing Blues," their 1949 hit with Little Esther.

Even though rock and roll remained at most a rumbling undercurrent in the Main Street record shops, the teen audience wasn't ignored. Hearthrob Eddie Fisher had four consecutive 1952 releases — "White Christmas," "You're All I Need for Christmas," "Here Comes Santa Claus," and "Jingle Bells" — all of which appeared on *Christmas with Eddie Fisher,* his RCA Victor LP issued the same year. Novelty records thrived throughout

the fifties. The season's most significant novelty came from Bugs Bunny voicemeister Mel Blanc, who brought Elmer Fudd to disc with "I Tan't Wait till Quithmuth," which was released in 1951 and reissued every year until 1954. Meanwhile, Howdy Doody returned with "Howdy Doody's Christmas Party" on RCA Victor's child-oriented Little Nipper label. Both Blanc and Doody also returned in 1952, with Mel waxing "Yeah, Das Is Ein Christmas Tree," while Howdy offered "A Howdy Doody Christmas."

Although they may have seemed like a novelty at the time, the Weavers, the first commercial folk group, inaugurated a new genre with their three 1951 releases, "We Wish You a Merry Christmas," "Poor Little Jesus," and "God Rest Ye Merry, Gentlemen." By 1952 folk buyers could also choose between two Decca LPs, the Weavers' *We Wish You a Merry Christmas,* which came out in 1951, and Burl Ives's *Christmas Day in the Morning.* Thanks to McCarthyism, which saw Ives squealing while the Weavers took the more heroic posture and clammed up, this first wave of the folk boom didn't last long. But it did establish that the folk audience preferred long-players to 45s — important market research for the real dawn of the folk boom, which came a few years later, after the Red Scare had died down.

In 1952 two New Orleans vocalists celebrated the season: Larry Darnell, with "Christmas Blues," and veteran jazz great Louis Armstrong, with "Winter Wonderland," his earliest known Christmas release. The same year, LA pianist Lloyd Glenn released "Sleigh Ride." Leroy Anderson originally wrote the song as an instrumental. After Glenn showed that the bright hoofbeat rhythm had hit potential, Mitchell Parrish added lyrics (just as he'd done several decades before to Hoagy Carmichael's melody for "Stardust") and the song hit vocally the same year as a duet for Bing Crosby and Peggy Lee.

But the definitive Christmas song of 1952 was the first release by a young unknown. Jimmy Boyd's "I Saw Mommy Kissing Santa Claus" was an easy number-one hit. It was covered by Teresa Brewer, immediately lampooned by Spike Jones (whose "All I Want for Christmas (Is My Two Front Teeth)" probably helped inspire it), then further parodied by country jokesters Homer and Jethro as "I Saw Mommy Smoochin' Santa Claus" in 1953. The Boyd original was kept in reissue print through 1955, the year the song was redone by Perry Como.

Not surprisingly, the following Christmas saw the Jimmy Boyd LP *Christmas with Boyd,* which was retitled *I Saw Mommy Kissing Santa Claus* in 1954, an indication that his Christmas hit wasn't at first perceived as the major (the only) reason for Boyd's success, even though today it's all anybody remembers about him. That's because Boyd had established himself as a significant child star of the period, landing a number of small hits, including several with Gayla Peevey, whose "I Want a Hippopotamus for Christmas," one of Dr. Demento's more enduring obscurities, further enlivened 1953. Christmas pop albums began to be marketed in earnest with Como's RCA LP *Around the Christmas Tree*. The label also put out Jack Webb's *The Christmas Story*. Webb, who created his Sgt. Joe Friday character on radio's "Dragnet," then carried it over to TV, didn't use that alter ego on this work. But Stan Freberg took care of that omission.

In 1953 Freberg and company proved the power of an excellent Joe Friday parody with "Christmas Dragnet," a skit that was retitled "Yulnet" in 1954. Several rhythm-and-blues takeoffs on the exceptionally popular "Dragnet," with its distinctive dramatic theme music, were forced off the market in 1953 because of supposed copyright problems. Freberg merely altered the title, though it's not known if infringement problems were the reason.

That same year, one of doowop's greatest records (and one of the rarest and most valuable Christmas records of all time) appeared: the lovely Moonglows ballad "Just a Lonely Christmas," backed with the equally fine jump side "Hey Santa Claus." It was a full year before the group found "Sincerely," but their skills already had matured. Meanwhile, Billy Ward and the Dominoes featured the lead of Jackie Wilson, who'd recently replaced Clyde McPhatter, on the overly orchestrated "Christmas in Heaven." In other rhythm-and-blues events

of note, Louis Armstrong returned with "Cool Yule."

Perhaps the season's most important Christmas debut came from Armenian-American songwriter Ross Bagdasarian, who released "Let's Have a Merry Merry Christmas." As David Seville, Bagdasarian later became Christmas's most important novelty innovator and character creator. In 1958 Bagdasarian assumed his new name and went to number one with "Witch Doctor," then used the voices from that release to create a new group, the Chipmunks.

The year finished out with Dean Martin crooning his way past his only holiday effort of the decade, "The Christmas Blues," a disc that would not necessarily have passed Muddy Waters' scrutiny for fitness with the genre. Meanwhile, the about-to-fade Jimmy Boyd attempted to reclaim the heights with his "Santa Claus Is Coming to Town" remake, while Les Paul reprised "White Christmas" as a six-string instrumental. Country Christmas activities held firm with two holiday first-timers, Hank Snow's romping "Reindeer Boogie" and newcomer Faron Young's "You're the Angel in My Christmas Tree." But country audiences are ever faithful to their heroes, and several veterans returned — notably Gene Autry, with the innocent (compared to the Ella Fitzgerald original) "Santa Claus Got Stuck in My Chimney." Red Foley recommended "Put Christ Back into Christmas," while Jimmy Wakely, not heard at holiday time since the 1940s, reminded his fans, "It's Christmas." On the R&B crooner side, Tommy Edwards upped the stakes with "It's Christmas Once Again," and Nat Cole went for the pop buyer with "The Little Boy Santa Claus Forgot," a real family values plea. (Santa forgot the kid because "he hasn't got a daddy," which seems to contradict the old gent's basic principles.)

The little-known Phil Moore Four came up with the rhythm-and-blues novelty "Stingy Old Scrooge," an urban folk story with a storyline similar to Babs

Gonzales' 1956 hit, "Be Bop Santa Claus."

The most seriously sensual Christmas disc of 1953, and perhaps of all time, came as Eartha Kitt purred her paean to bipolar lust, "Santa Baby," a sensation she tried to repeat through the next several holiday seasons, notably with "This Year's Santa Baby" in

1954, the same year that "Santa Baby" was parodied by Homer and Jethro.

Otherwise, 1954 proved a slow year for parodies, although "Honeymooners" TV comic Art Carney recorded "Santa and the Doodle-Li-Boop" and Spike Jones came up with "I Want Eddie Fisher for Christmas," which set the mold for similar titles in years to come.

Country was also poorly represented in 1954, with just two records of note: the Davis Sisters' "Christmas Boogie" and Terry Fell's attempt to cash in on the then-current mambo craze, "We Wanna See Santa Do the Mambo."

In August of 1953, Nat Cole went back into the studio under the supervision of Nelson Riddle to record a new version of "The Christmas Song" to completely replace the original 1946 version. That first version had already been altered with dubbed-in strings for Christmas of 1948 and it was that doctored rendition that had been on the market between 1948 and Christmas of 1952.

In that he had only recently joined

Capitol, Riddle did not receive label credit ("with string choir" was how the label read). This new release on the Capitol Christmas 90000 series, was the sweetened version that remained in print throughout the decade, placed in reissue in both 1954 and 1956.

Capitol's other major vocalist, Frank Sinatra, had recorded a 1944 cover of "White Christmas," on Columbia. Capitol

had Sinatra redo the song, which was issued in tandem with Cole's remake. Decca countered with another "White Christmas" remake, this time putting Crosby together with Danny Kaye and Peggy Lee, in the apparent hope that three voices would be better than one. Decca also issued another Crosby Yule album, 1954's *White Christmas.*

Instrumentally, the record industry celebrated via two LPs, Percy Faith's *Music of Christmas,* a Columbia release that was reissued in 1959 when Faith was a number-one chartmaker with "Theme from a Summer Place," and Ferrante and Teicher's *Christmas Hi-Fi Favorites,* issued long before the piano duet hit big with "Exodus" and similarly lugubrious themes from high-profile movies.

But 1954 stands as the first glorious year for Christmas works by black vocal groups. In Philadelphia,

George Castelle — actually George Grant of the Castelles — recorded "It's Christmas Time," a song eventually reissued (and currently in release) under the Castelles name. On the West Coast, Little Esther and Mel Walker, two Johnny Otis regulars well past their early 1950s prime, recorded "My Christmas Blues," while Oscar McLollie and the Honeyjumpers, still hot from their 1953 hit, "The Honeyjump," returned with "Dig That Crazy Santa Claus."

There is no doubt, however, that the most important Christmas release of the year, and perhaps the decade, came from the group first assembled around Clyde McPhatter's clear, high tenor in 1952. McPhatter had been lead singer of Billy Ward's Dominoes since 1950, and though he sang only background in their biggest hit, "Sixty-Minute Man," from 1951, his style and clarity were forced to the front in 1952's "Have Mercy Baby." Clearly, McPhatter possessed star power, and manager George Treadwell snapped him up as eagerly as Atlantic Records bought the group from Treadwell.

As Clyde McPhatter and the Drifters (the name was chosen because group members had drifted in from various groups), the guys struck gold with their 1953 rocker "Money Honey," followed by the sensual Latin-based plum "Honey Love." "White Christmas," along with

Ten Best Doowop Christmas Records

1. The Youngsters, "Christmas in Jail"
(This one could also easily make number one on the novelty list.)

2. The Moonglows, "Just a Lonely Christmas" / "Hey Santa Claus"
(Both sides — a tie for number two.)

3. The Orioles,
"What Are You Doing New Year's Eve"

4. The Ravens, "White Christmas"

5. The Cadillacs, "Rudolph the Red-Nosed Reindeer"
(Our boy Rudy's never swung so fine, before or since.)

6. The Shells, "Happy Holiday"

7. The Orioles, "Lonely Christmas"

8. The Drifters, "The Christmas Song"
(The group's second great Christmas disc, this one with Johnny Moore taking the lead vocal.)

9. Oscar McLollie and the Honeyjumpers, "Dig That Crazy Santa Claus"

10. Nathaniel Mayer and the Fabulous Twilights, "Mr. Santa Claus"

that other Crosby-identified standard, "The Bells of St. Mary's," was recorded in the same late-1953 session as "Honey Love" and "Whatcha Gonna Do," an uptempo song that influenced "The Twist." The Christmas tunes were held for release until Yuletide 1954. When the popularity of this harmony-rich remake became obvious, Mercury reissued the 1948 Ravens version, on which the

Drifters' arrangement was based, in an effort to cover — that is, kill off in favor of their own product — the Drifters' hit. Didn't matter — the Drifters, with Bill Pinckney's deep bass lead at the top and McPhatter's crying lead at the climax, proved indomitable. As much or more than any of their regular R&B releases, "White Christmas" defined the Clyde McPhatter and the Drifters style, and the record stayed in the Atlantic singles catalog for as long as singles were issued. And Irving Berlin never even complained about the harmonic license the group took with his biggest song — a position he would not maintain the next time someone rocked it up.

The L.A.–based Penguins' major success was "Earth Angel," a song drawn from the talents of Jesse Belvin and other group voices on the black-oriented Hollywood scene in the early 1950s. On the strength of this hit, Mercury Records bought the group's contract from the black-owned Dootone label. At the

same time, manager Buck Ram's other group, the Platters, were signed as a "throw-in." Mercury immediately began grooming the Penguins as America's next big R&B crossover group, but the makeover didn't take. The records were fine, but whenever one was played on the radio, the original "Earth Angel" tended to start selling again, not the new release — it was as if the Penguins covered themselves. Even their Christmas release, the ballad "A Christmas Prayer" backed with the up-tempo "Jingle Jangle," fizzled. (The Platters, thanks to spectacular tenor lead Tony Williams, bailed out Mercury's investment.)

Another Los Angeles vocal group, the Hollywood Flames, had been recording since 1950, though they lacked a major success until 1957's "Buzz Buzz Buzz." In 1955, the Voices, an offshoot Flames group headed by Bobby Byrd, later famous as Bobby Day, with "Rock-In Robin," recorded a double-sided Christmas release, "Santa

Claus Baby" backed with "Santa Claus Boogie." Byrd/Day chose the band's name because the sides' harmonies were primarily created with the then-novel tactic of

multiply tracking his voice.

A third 1954 doowop Christmas release came from the New York City group the Valentines, a group led by

Richard Barrett. Barrett, the man who nurtured, if he cannot quite be said to have discovered, both Frankie Lymon of the Teenagers and Arlene Smith of the Chantels, came up with his own "Christmas Prayer" in 1955. Unlike earlier Valentines releases, "Woo Woo Train" and "Lily Mae-belle," this Christmas effort didn't have a prayer.

For a record-store-based series of tiny labels, the Jackson Trio made "Jingle Bell Hop," while Chet Atkins put an instrumental spin on "Jingle Bells" for the giant RCA Victor, both in 1955. The same year, Louis Armstrong deployed his singular talents on a reprise of "Christmas Night in Harlem," the 1934 original by Clarence Williams, with whom Armstrong once played.

It was also in 1955 that Jimmy Boyd tried to put a contemporary teen spin on Autry's 1949 hit with "Reindeer Rock." It was Boyd's final holiday effort, though he's been around ever since

anyway, thanks to catching Mom and Santa in that clinch.

The pop crooning that Crosby initiated in the thirties was also stumbling along on its last legs. Perry Como, riding high with a series of holiday television specials, gave Christmas records a final try with his version of "'Twas the Night Before Christmas," a release that came out on the Bluebird Children's label at the same time that Como was enjoying major pop hits on the parent label, RCA Victor. Another smooth crooner, Andy Williams, came up with his first holiday release, "Christmas Is a Feeling in Your Heart," on Cadence, years before he went to Columbia and years before he made Christmas TV specials his full-time career.

In 1955 RCA Victor made a major move on the Christmas novelty market with the Singing Dogs' version of "Jin-gle Bells." A taste of Chipmunks to come? Hardly. Rumor has it that these were real dogs with a real ability to bark on tune, more or less. Before you get too carried away speculating whether record buyers in 1955 suffered from a mass case of bad taste, remember that these are the same dogs that generate requests, dedications, and generally a lot of play on current Christmas retrospectives on contemporary rock-and-roll radio.

Perhaps the most covered, though least remembered, Christmas novelty was produced in late 1955. Originally by Joe Ward, the child's plaint "Nuttin' for Christmas" somehow captured the imagination of record buyers and record companies most everywhere, prompting covers by Ricky Zahnd, the Fontane Sisters, Barry Gordon and Art Mooney, and even Eartha Kitt, in addition to parodies by Stan Freberg and the ubiquitous Homer and Jethro (whose travesty was titled "Hurtin' for Christmas").

Chapter Three

Jingle Bell Rock

Christmas Gets the Beat

THE HIT PARADE of the late fifties remained steeped in eclecticism. As had been true since the end of World War II, just about anything could become a hit. But a central theme now began emerging: the rise of rock and roll from the heart of rhythm and blues. Early rock and roll deserved every bit of its reputation as the most rebellious and uncouth form of pop music ever heard. But that didn't stop even the wildest rockers from celebrating the joys of the Christmas season, although, like each new group before them, rock-and-rollers brought their own customs and perspectives to the party.

Certainly in 1956, the pop world's two most arresting developments were Elvis Presley and "Heartbreak Hotel." Nothing came close. Not Carl Perkins's "Blue Suede Shoes,"

not "My Prayer" by the Platters, and especially not "Please Please Please," James Brown and the Famous Flames' first record — that one didn't even crack the national top 100.

Something about the latest major phenomenon attracts a whole universe of imitators, emulators, and wanna-bes. So 1956 saw a variety of Elvis references and rip-offs, some of which had a Christmas spin. One of the best known was Little Lambsie Penn's "I Want to Spend Christmas with Elvis" for Atco, the label that songwriter Bobby Darin (presently recording for Decca) joined in 1957. Marlene Paul recorded a variation on the same theme, changing the spelling (to "I Want to Spend Xmas with Elvis"), but not the meaning. The Holly Twins (no known connection with Buddy, this vocal did use the voice of a little-known and uncredited Eddie Cochran supplying the impersonation of Presley doing something that sounded like "Don't Be Cruel") recorded a third variation, "I Want Elvis for Christmas" on the recently established Liberty label. But the Holly Twins received neither the Memphis Flash nor even a spot on the charts when they unwrapped that year's gifts.

Plenty of others also took a crack at chipping off a shard of Presley's crown. Mad Milo's "Elvis for Christmas" was done "break-in" style — in which one- or two-second snippets of popular records are patched together (often as "quotes") to tell a topical story of sorts, an idea popularized (and practically perfected) by Buchanan and Goodman's "Flying Saucer" in 1956. But Buchanan and Goodman didn't get around to Christmas until 1957's "Santa and the Satellite." They never got around to breaking-in Elvis.

Lalo Guerrero's take on Elvis was the very spoofy, very ethnic "Elvis Perez," the flip of which, "Pancho Claus," was part of a series of Los Angeles–based Guerrero parodies. Best known for his "Pound Dog," a lampoon of Elvis's "Hound Dog," Guerrero's recordings can be traced back to 1950 with "Marijuana Boogie," which became

---

FIVE BEST ROCKABILLY CHRISTMAS RECORDS

1. Bobby Helms, "Jingle Bell Rock" (Even the 1961 Chubby Checker–Bobby Rydell Bandstand remake of this 1957 original was good, or at least better than the average Philadelphia pop hit.)

2. Brenda Lee, "Rockin' Around the Christmas Tree"

3. Chuck Berry, "Run Rudolph Run"

4. Elvis Presley, "Santa Claus Is Back in Town"

5. Three Aces and a Joker, "Sleigh Bell Rock"

---

the danceable sound track of the play and movie *Zoot Suit,* and forward through the 1980s.

The definitive Christmas release of 1957, however influenced by Elvis it

obviously was, never mentioned his name: Bobby Helms's "Jingle Bell Rock." The new song followed up Bobby's top-ten ballad "My Special Angel" and gave rockabilly its most recognizable Christmas classic. No one since has ever successfully put a "boogie" or a "hop" tag to "Jingle Bells," though several instrumentalists, including Bobby Rey ("Rockin' J Bells" in 1958) and Santo and Johnny ("Twistin' Bells" in 1960), have tried. "Jingle Bell Rock" has become a classic. Its genial guitar figures and light nonsense lyrics ("giddy up, jingle horse, pick up your feet/jingle around the block") bring a cheerful note to each new Christmas season.

Chubby Checker and Bobby Rydell did get additional hit mileage out of their 1961 remake of "Jingle Bell Rock," a song from which they excised the rockabilly feel in favor of the friendly Philly teen-dance pop sound, at once soulless and ubiquitous.

The 1956 urban folktale "Be Bop Santa Claus," by singer Babs Gonzales, is a supercool, superhip take on a Harlem Santa. Recorded for at least two labels — Bruce of New York, and King, the major rhythm-and-blues label from Cincinnati — the Gonzales release just keeps on being popular. A similar theme can be traced back to the Phil Moore Four's "Stingy Old Scrooge" from 1953, although Gonzales, a bebop wildman who did everything from chauffeuring Errol Flynn to penning a couple of autobiographies, certainly seems capable of having come up with such a shaggy-dog story all on his own.

RCA Victor's Harry Belafonte recorded "Mary's Boy Child" in 1956, the first Christmas effort by the era's calypso superstar. Mahalia Jackson reprised "The Lord's Prayer" for Columbia in 1956, returning in 1957 with "Sweet Little Jesus Boy," both from her 1955 Columbia LP.

Los Angeles's doowop godfather, Jesse Belvin, had a major hit with "Goodnight My Love," a syrupy 1957 original. Belvin contributed a Yule tune to the B side, "I Want You with Me Xmas," but the ballad was as weak as his spelling. (Jesse sang "Christmas," not "Xmas," of course.)

Today, a rapper who sang about his experiences with drunk driving could count on getting his hands slapped, if he weren't banned altogether. But in the mid-fifties, drunk driving hadn't yet become a gravely humorless social concern, so the Youngsters were able to get away with "Christmas in Jail." The track was originally the flip side of "Dreamy Eyes," their 1956 hit. Once 1957 arrived and Santa departed, "Christmas in Jail" was replaced by "I'm Sorry Now," so that the Youngsters could continue to compete against the Four Preps' version of "Dreamy Eyes." But "Christmas in Jail" proved the most enduring side of the bunch. And all the frivolity aside, the tale is a cautionary one — drunk drivers went to jail back then, too, and for Christmas dinner, "they gave me lots of bread and water to drink."

Recording for the Philadelphia-based Cameo label, the Cameos came up with a clever double-sided holiday release: "Merry Christmas" on the A side, "Happy New Year's" on the B side. From Detroit came the Falcons, the group that launched the careers of Wilson Pickett, Eddie Floyd, and Sir Mack Rice. Floyd and Rice were members when the Falcons recorded "Can This Be Christmas" in 1957. There was no response, most

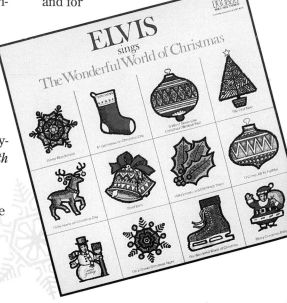

"Speedoo," from which the lead singer, Earl Carroll, took his Speedoo nickname (not the other way around, no matter what the lyric claims). And in 1956, the Cadillacs got their Christmas chance with a novelty doowop version of Autry's classic, "Rudolph the Red-Nosed Reindeer." It's not as memorable as their earlier hits — or as Autry's — but the very idea of rearranging the song is bold, the kind of thing that so annoyed rock-and-roll haters — and delighted aficionados — of the period. And it sold.

Based on the success of the Cadillacs' "Rudolph" reprise, Gene Autry decided to remake his original hit from 1949 on his own newly founded Challenge label, backed with a new rendition of his Christmas-of-1947 hit "Here Comes Santa Claus." Accompanying these was an LP, *Christmastime with Gene Autry.* Autry recognized that by keeping both songs in its permanent catalog, Columbia was making far more money than the artist, whose royalties

were a small fraction of profits. Now that he owned his own record company, Autry made money as both artist and owner — enough to buy radio stations, TV stations, even a major-league baseball franchise. *'Tis* the season to be jolly.

Another performer with major country credentials was George Jones, whose first regular effort, for Starday, came out in 1955. Jones also did pseudonymous rockabilly for Starday as Thumper Jones and for

likely
because few record
buyers heard the question, even in the Motor City. Their major success came in 1959, when the Falcons issued "You're So Fine," one of soul's very best releases ever; it went top twenty nationwide.

In 1954, the Cadillacs debuted with the glorious doowop ballad "Gloria"; in 1955, they hit with the novelty

Tops as Hank Smith. But country was Jones's true passion, and true gift, as he showed frequently over the years, including on "New Baby for Christmas," his 1957 Mercury-label Christmas release.

Among those whose Christmas releases were LPs rather than singles (a sign of how much the market for the new record format had developed) were Joni James, with *Merry Christmas from Joni* on MGM, *Christmas Eve with Burl Ives* on Decca, and *Spike Jones Presents a Christmas Spectacular* on Verve. Retitled *Let's Sing a Song of Christmas* in 1961, the latter is an inspired rampage of cacophony by any name.

Other notable LPs of the 1957 season included *Teresa Brewer at Christmas Time* on Coral, Bing Crosby's *That Christmas Feeling* on Decca, and Frank Sinatra's *A Jolly Christmas* on Capitol, which was reissued a decade later as *The Frank Sinatra Christmas Album* to compete with a 1967 release, *Frank Sinatra Christmas Album,* on Sinatra's own Reprise label. And in 1958, Harry Belafonte's *To Wish You a Merry Christmas* on RCA Victor and Tennessee Ernie Ford's *The Star Carol* on Capitol were joined by *Greetings from the McGuire Sisters* on Coral.

There was one crucial Christmas long-player released in 1957. Elvis came up with one of the definitive Christmas LPs, *Elvis' Christmas Album,* packaged with a spectacular gatefold cover that included fan photos of Presley. The LP was reissued on RCA Camden in 1970 and stays in print on compact disc to this day. A single from the LP, "Blue Christmas," was issued in promo form in 1957, commercially in 1964.

Elvis didn't put out "White Christmas" as a single. But his advent had so disordered the Tin Pan Alley brain trust that when Irving Berlin heard Elvis's version of his most cherished (and profitable) icon, he ordered his staff to phone radio stations around the country to demand that they cease airing it. This extraordinary effort — as ineffectual as it was petulant — shows mainly how far out of touch Berlin, like so many of his show tune peers, had become with what was happening in popular music. If ol' Irving had ever heard the version by Clyde McPhatter and the Drifters, of which Elvis's remake was an exceedingly gentle replay, he probably would have fainted dead away.

Johnny Mathis returned pop crooning to the fore in 1957; though he didn't have a Christmas single until the 1960s, Mathis got a quick start with the permanently popular *Merry Christmas* on Columbia in 1958. The renewed interest in crooning was not missed by Roulette Records, the New York label that introduced the first doowop crossover record, "Why Do Fools Fall in Love" by Frankie Lymon and the Teenagers, in 1955. Lymon was tabbed to be an ex–Teenagers lead from the very start, it was just a question of when. By 1957, he was already recording as a single. "It's Christmas Once Again" was an attempt to give Lymon a pop identity before he'd turned sixteen. It failed to return him to the top ten, as did every succeeding Lymon record. By age twenty-six, rock and roll's first great actual teenager had died of a heroin overdose.

Christmas diversity — the whole Santa's bag of pop, novelty, and rock and roll — reached its pinnacle in 1958. In that one holiday season, it seemed, Christmas music exploded. There was no form it did not take — including the ancient, or at least quasi-ancient. For that was the year that the Harry Simeone Chorale recorded "The Little Drummer Boy," an original composition — written by Simeone with Katherine Davis and Henry Onorati — that sounded like a legitimate throwback to 1928, or even 1858.

Equally timeless is the lyrical story-line about a poor little boy who journeys to Bethlehem to share with the Christ child his only treasure, an ability to play the snare drum.

The original stayed in print through 1963, though Simeone also remade the song on occasion. So did Johnny Cash in 1959, Johnny Mathis in 1963, Joan Baez in 1966, both Kenny Burrell and Lou Rawls in 1967, Emmylou Harris in 1980, and David Bowie with Bing Crosby in 1982. With its paradiddle rhythms, dramatic bolero-style crescendo, and the throbbing hum of its vocal background arrangement, "The Little Drummer Boy" also attracted the likes of hard rockers Jimi Hendrix, Joan Jett in 1981, and Bob Seger and the Silver Bullet Band in 1987. Simeone's accompanying LP was a pop-choral masterpiece, featuring traditional carols and originals in lively, varied arrangements. It was released on 20th Fox in 1958 as *Sing We Now of Christ-*

mas and was retitled *The Little Drummer Boy* in 1963, by which time it was abundantly clear that the title was a permanent fixture of the season. In 1968 and again in 1976, NBC turned "The Little Drummer Boy" into a thirty-minute Christmas TV special; both featured the same narrator, Greer Garson, with plot embellishments involving everything from gypsy kidnappers to Roman tax collectors.

In 1958, instrumentalists' albums proliferated with Billy Vaughn's *Christmas Carols* on Dot, Percy Faith's *Hallelujah* on Columbia, and rhythm-and-blues' earliest holiday LP, Bill Doggett's *Songs of Christmas,* on King.

Brenda Lee made her first record at age twelve (though her record company claimed she was nine) and her first Christmas record, "I'm Gonna Lasso Santa Claus," in 1956. That cheerfully demented disc was the first rockabilly Christmas release ever, and quickly graduated Lee from Decca's children's series to its adult pop line. Although

---

Ten Best Christmas Blues Records

1. John Lee Hooker, "Blues for Christmas"
2. Lowell Fulson, "Lonesome Christmas"
3. Lightning Hopkins, "Merry Christmas"
4. Chuck Berry, "Merry Christmas, Baby" (tied with)
   Elvis Presley, "Merry Christmas, Baby"
6. Freddy King, "I Hear Jingle Bells"
7. Big Maybelle, "White Christmas"
8. Floyd Dixon, "Empty Stocking Blues"
9. B. B. King, "Christmas Celebration"
10. The Eagles, "Please Come Home for Christmas"

---

her biggest pop successes, "Sweet Nothin's" in 1959 and "Emotions" in 1960, were yet to come, and although

the rockabilly style was fading, Christmas 1958 found Lee's stocking once more stuffed with enough rockin' rhythm for her to produce the celebrated "Rockin' Around the Christmas Tree." This R&B-inflected jaunt has kept Brenda Lee's joyful, catchy voice on the radio year after year for more than three decades as a Christmas perennial.

Columbia Records might have thought they could pass Little Cindy and her "Happy Birthday Jesus" off as a Brenda Lee clone. Well, Little Cindy was no Brenda Lee, but she did make one of the most ludicrous Christmas releases of all time. "Happy Birthday Jesus" begins with a male voice setting up the vocal, then what sounds like a preteen girl with a thick Southern accent in recitation, while an intrusive choir hums "Silent Night." Yech.

Gospel's Pilgrim Travelers quartet, who'd recorded Crosby's "I'll Be Home for Christmas" in 1953, briefly became the Travelers, with Lou Rawls now a member of the group, for a few pop releases five years later. Under that name, they were able to give the same Crosby-originated material another try for the Andex label. Specialty Records quickly responded to its small hint of sales power by reissuing the Pilgrim Travelers' 1953 recording.

Longtime Los Angeles session man Bobby Rey had been kicking around the local scene as a member of the Masked Phantom Band, the house band at the legendary El Monte Legion Stadium rock-and-roll shows. "Rockin' J Bells," Rey's Latin-tinged takeoff on "Jingle Bells," was backed with "Corrido Auld Lang Syne" and became a Los Angeles holiday favorite in 1958. From another barrio, Augie Rios turned out a national hit with the kiddie novelty "Donde Esta Santa Claus"; the question was strong enough to be repeated on a 1964 reissue. In 1966, LA's Salas Brothers, who later created the rock band Tierra, again redid this Spanish-language holiday classic, whose appeal marks a rare example of anglophone American audiences transcending a language barrier. But then, "Where Is Santa Claus?" is a universal sentiment as the hour grows late on December 24.

Beyond any doubt, there were more novelty hits in 1958 than in any other year on record, and this was doubly — perhaps trebly — true as the holidays approached. Yet neither Jim Backus with "Why Don't You Go Home for Christmas?" nor the Mickey Mouse Club's "Christmas Theme of Disneyland" generated much sales. Backus, whose voice became Mr. Magoo's on the popular TV cartoon series, had already hit that year with "Delicious," a fairly funny skit about drinking, hiccuping, then drinking some more. The mees-ka, moose-ka, Mouseketeers had daily afternoon TV exposure. Both must have seemed like naturals for the Christmas hit parade. They flopped regardless.

Satirist Stan Freberg hadn't done Christmas since "Christmas Dragnet" in 1953. Five years later, he was just as funny, but meaner — probably because he hated both rock and roll, which now saturated the airwaves, and advertising, the field in which he now found himself making a living. His calculated seasonal satire, "Green Christma$," a 1958 hit that was reissued in 1972, may be the most merciless Christmas noise anybody's made since Scrooge changed his tune. But, though

(Wooley, who went on to a distinguished career as a Nashville songwriter, finished 1958 with a remake of "Here Comes Santa Claus.")

To enter Christmas lore on an all-too-permanent basis, all Seville needed to do was take the same sped-up voices that sang "walla walla bing bang" in "Witch Doctor" and give them a new identity. Rather than identifying them as salivating cannibals, he called them the Chipmunks and released "The Chipmunk Song," a 1958 number-one record that sold for decades. It also salvaged Liberty Records, whose chipmunks of . . . er, *chairmen* of the board were none other than Simon (Warnoker), and Alvin (Bennett), along with Theodore (Keep), chief engineer. The Chipmunks went on to win a Grammy for best children's recording of 1958. Seville made several other Chipmunks records, and his creation was revived in the eighties, to make disco

there's little pleasure in reporting it, the definitive Christmas novelty of 1958 came from David Seville (aka Ross Bagdasarian). Seville had already hit number one with "Witch Doctor" the previous summer, but he can be forgiven that, for it was the inspiration for the bizarre eloquence of Sheb Wooley's "The Purple People Eater."

records, country-and-western albums, and a TV series, all with voices recorded normally and played back at warp speed.

The Chipmunks were so successful that they inevitably spawned imitators, especially since anyone with a multi-speed tape deck could achieve the same effect as Alvin and the boys. Capitol Records was early in picking up the Chipmunks' cudgel with "The Happy Reindeer," by Dancer Prancer and Nervous, an actual 1959 hit.

It was in 1959 that ABC-TV, proprietors of a Friday-night TV private eye show called *77 Sunset Strip,* and the Warner Bros. label (a then-tiny enterprise that's now the world's most dominant recording force) decided to cash in on the popularity of Edd "Kookie" Byrnes, the slang-dripping Hollywood parking-lot jockey featured on the show. His silly "Kookie, Kookie, Lend Me Your Comb," a duet with Connie Stevens, had considerable chart success. To follow up, Byrnes's "Yulesville" was put on the market for the Christmas season, accompanied by a holiday 45 from *77 Sunset Strip* leading man Efrem Zimbalist, Jr., who gave a really profound reading to

"Adeste Fidelis," in the deep bass tones later familiar to millions from his seventies series *The FBI.* Though neither song hit, thus came the future monolith Warner Bros. to the Christmas marketplace.

Jim Backus, relentless in his Mr. Magoo persona as he'd never been as James Dean's father in *Rebel Without a Cause,* gave Christmas one more try with "I Was a Teenage Reindeer," but it bore no more fruit than his 1958 effort. Jimmie Rodgers, a pop-folk singer who had success with "Honeycomb" in 1957 and "Secretly" in 1958, ended 1959

with "It's Christmas Once Again," the title of both his single and his LP.

It's now well known that the original Drifters were fired in 1959 by their manager, George Treadwell, who owned the name and therefore could do stuff like that. It's equally widely known that the Five Crowns, led by Ben E. King, were hired to fill a Drifters' engagement at the Apollo Theater, and did so well that they were then hired to record "There Goes My Baby," their number-two hit in 1959. But where did the fired Drifters drift? The answer came at Christmas: They became the Harmony Grits, a group that had two releases for the End label (fitting, isn't it?), one of them a new R&B "Santa Claus Is Coming to Town" in 1959. It drifted precisely nowhere, certainly nowhere near the charts.

If you've been dreaming of a Black Christmas, jump into the wayback machine and set the controls for 1959. Redd Foxx recorded "Christmas Hard Times" for LA's Dootone label, and

Pearl Bailey tried "Jingle Bells Cha Cha," backed with a memorable hymn to Mammon, "Five-Pound Box of Money," for Roulette in 1959. In other R&B-related Yule news, Dinah Washington offered up "Ol Santa," while her duet partner Brook Benton came forth with "This Time of the Year," a 1959 success that was repackaged and reissued every year from 1960 to 1963. Benton's disc competes with the 1955 Solomon Burke effort "Christmas Presents" as the earliest Christmas record whose style can legitimately be termed "soul."

In 1964, Aretha Franklin — and in Nashville, Brenda Lee — gave voice to "Winter Wonderland." But it was an instrumental version of that song that proved most long-lasting. The Ramsey Lewis Trio's "Winter Wonderland" was their first attempt at giving Christmas a jazz feel, as well as the first of many holiday classics redone by the Chicago-based jazz pianist and his combo. Lewis recorded for Argo, the jazz arm of the Windy City's historic Chess Records combine. When Chess renamed Argo Cadet in 1965, the label reissued Lewis's "Winter Wonderland," and in the wake of his huge instrumental hit with "The 'In' Crowd," it took on new life, leading to a series of Trio Christmas albums.

But 1959's real Christmas classic came from none other than Chuck Berry — his first and his best attempt at capturing the season in song. Berry backed an effectively bluesy cover of "Merry Christmas Baby" with a delightful, romping son-of-"Rudolph the Red-Nosed Reindeer" he called "Run Rudolph Run" (though he sang "Run, run, Rudolph"). The song became a guitar slinger's standard, redone in decades to come by the Berry-worshiping likes of Keith Richards, Dave Edmunds, and Bryan Adams.

But not all of 1959's seasonal heroes came from the newfangled ranks of rock and roll or R&B. Even ten years after "Rudolph" first reigned, Gene Autry stayed busy, this time recording another attempt at a new Rudolph, "Santa's Comin' in a Whirlybird" for Republic.

Record companies now realized there was a steady holiday market for LPs of Christmas music by almost any of their hitmakers. Many of these records sound as if they were churned out on assignment, but just about every charting artist of the period had to make at least a nodding acquaintance with carols and standards. Among those checking in for 1959 was Pat Boone, with *White Christmas* on Dot (his earliest Christmas release of several, it was retitled *Christmas Is a Comin'* when reissued in 1966). *Seasons Greetings from Perry Como* came out on RCA Victor that year, while Dean Martin's *A Winter Romance* appeared on Capitol (it was retitled *Holiday Cheer* in 1965). The Mills Brothers' *Merry Christmas* was also issued on Dot, and Connie Francis's *Christmas in My Heart* on MGM.

It was now almost twenty years since the musical revolution wrought by "White Christmas." Christmas songs had evolved from an incidental part of a sheet music–centered industry into an important element in a record-based music business. Even the technology had been transformed, going from 78s to 45s to 33⅓-rpm LPs. In the coming decade, however, things would be turned upside down in ways that never entered the heads of Crosby or Berlin — or Santa himself.

Chapter Four

A Christmas Gift for You

Phil Spector and the End of Christmas Past

*J*UST AS they eradicated so much else, the sixties wiped out what was left of Christmas Past. Yuletide hits still occurred regularly, but with rare exception, they had less impact than their predecessors from the forties and fifties. Nevertheless, the sixties represents the apex of rock-and-roll and rhythm-and-blues achievement, and when memorable Christmas music was created, it tended to rank with the best of all time.

The decade was legendarily slow in getting started in almost every area (some don't date the first "sixties rock" until 1962 or 1963), and holiday music proved no exception. No classic Christmas works emerged from the winter of 1960. From a chart perspective, the clear winners were those darned Chipmunks, who placed their "Rudolph the Red-Nosed Reindeer" at number twenty-one. Little else even charted.

The Statues, a white doowop group from Nashville (some members of which later formed Ronny and the Daytonas — remember 1964's "Little GTO"?), came up with yet another version of "White Christmas" in 1960. It was quickly followed by the third reissue of the song by the Ravens, this time on the Savoy label. A New York–area vocal group, the Shells, recorded the excellent, up-tempo "Happy Holiday" for that season. During the doowop revival of 1961, the Shells charted their original 1957 version of "Baby Oh Baby" for the very first time. But "Happy Holiday" never had so much as a glimmer of such success.

Rock-oriented artists with greater chart success also tried their luck with holiday releases during late 1960. Among them were Danny and the Juniors, who had gone a long spell since their 1958 number-one success with "At the Hop." Their 1960 effort "Candy Cane, Sugary Plum" continued their streak by denting no charts. The steel-guitar-based instrumental duet Santo and Johnny attempted to parlay their 1959 "Sleep Walk" success into

"Twistin' Bells," an instrumental knock-off of "Jingle Bells," in 1960. They did chart into the top fifty, just barely.

Recording stars making the transition to the still-massive saloon-singer circuit had bigger hits. Bobby Darin, who first hit with "Splish Splash" in 1958 on his way to becoming one of the biggest pop singers rock created, charted both his "Christmas Auld Lang Syne" as well as the flip, "Child of God." Paul Anka, who hit number one with his earliest chart hit, "Diana," in 1957, couldn't do the same with his remake of Jimmy Boyd's "I Saw Mommy Kissing Santa Claus" or its flip side, "Rudolph the Red-Nosed Reindeer." He compensated by writing "The Tonight Show" theme with Johnny Carson, "My Way," for big-league egomaniacs from Sinatra on down, and "Having My Baby" for himself and whoever wants it. The same year, both stars put out Christmas LPs — Anka *It's Christmas Everywhere* and Darin *The 25th Day of December with Bobby Darin*.

But for the most part, Christmas 1960 featured a purely miscellaneous batch of releases, good, bad, and indifferent, from artists across the same spectrum of quality. The great bluesman John Lee Hooker, on the Detroit-based Hi-Q (a subsidiary of the already minuscule Motown predecessor Fortune Records), came up with "Blues for Christmas," while Ron Holden, creator of the early Pacific Northwest

THE 25TH DAY OF DECEMBER WITH BOBBY DARIN

grunge classic "Love You So," recorded the downright weird "Who Says There Ain't No Santa Claus?" It is almost certainly the only Christmas ditty that ends with a visit to the electric chair.

Christmas of 1960 did bring forth a trio of jazz-based holiday LPs, though even these were relatively lackluster: Nat King Cole's *The Magic of Christmas* (reissued as *The Christmas Song* in 1963), Keely Smith's *A Keely Christmas*, and Ella Fitzgerald's *A Swinging Christmas* (retitled *Ella Wishes You a Swinging Christmas* in 1982). For the urban folk market, the Kingston Trio finished 1960 with *Last Month of the Year*.

Toward the end of 1961, it was clear that Chubby Checker, the man who charted "The Twist" at number one for two years in a row and limboed through a half dozen other dance hits in between, could have real impact for the holidays. He made the grade with his duet with Bobby Rydell on a remake of Bobby Helms's

"Jingle Bell Rock." The song charted at number twenty-one in 1961 and returned to *Billboard*'s Hot 100 the next year too. The B side, "Jingle Bells," featured both singers impersonating other artists, à la one of Checker's first hits, "The Class," a 1959 release in which he did pretty nice imitations of Fats Domino, Elvis, the Coasters, and those darned Chipmunks. Another 1961 remake of "Jingle Bells," by RCA Victor session guitarist (and longtime Elvis Presley producer) Chet Atkins, hit the market with considerably less impact; of equal note was its flip, none other than "Jingle Bell Rock." Bobby Darin released "O Come All Ye Faithful" as a single from his 1960 Christmas LP during this same season.

Chicago's great black crooner Jerry Butler released "O Holy Night," which was redone two years later by Detroit's original soul genius Jackie Wilson. (Pat Boone, nobody's idea of a soul expert, took on the same tune in 1963 also). Johnny Mathis chipped in with "My

Kind of Christmas." Longtime Oakland blues pianist and vocalist Jimmy McCracklin, best known for his 1958 dance hit "The Walk," followed his 1961 rhythm-and-blues success called "Just Got to Know" with "Christmas Time" for the small Art-Tone label. Meantime, the newly minted Motown label had one quickly forgotten holiday release, the Twistin'

Kings' "Christmas Twist," an instrumental. It was one of two Kings' instrumentals issued consecutively in late 1961, and among the few nonvocal recordings Berry Gordy and company ever released.

Dickie Goodman, famous for his "break-in" work with Buchanan and Goodman, made a series of three spoofs featuring "The Touchables," based on the popular *Untouchables* ABC-TV series about Elliot Ness and the G-men who put Al Capone and his crew out of business during Prohibition. The final installment was "Santa and the Touchables," which barely nudged into the top 100 in late 1961.

It was a California crooner whose Christmas career reached back into the 1940s who came up with the 1961 season's best holiday hope. Charles Brown's "Please Come Home for Christmas," its lyric very much reminiscent of "I'll Be Home for Christmas" viewed from the reverse angle, and its deep blues arrangement suggesting a much earlier period, captured major sales for that initial Christmas and for many Christmases to come. Coupled with "Merry Christmas Baby," "Please Come Home for Christmas," later recorded by virtually everybody from the lowliest blues singers to the Eagles when they were flying at their highest, gave Charles Brown a pair of the most recorded Yule favorites, and definitive claim to being the

greatest blues and R&B Christmas artist of all time. His first LP, *Charles Brown Sings Christmas Songs,* was issued in tandem with this release. In 1972 the album was retitled *Please Come Home for Christmas,* as it had become clear which of its songs really counted.

In the instrumental file, Ramsey Lewis's *The Sound of Christmas* was the first of the jazz pianist's several holiday albums, while Chet Atkins released *Christmas with Chet Atkins,* an LP sufficiently memorable to fans of the great Nashville guitarman to be reissued in 1976.

Like 1960, Christmas 1962 was a mixed bag of releases with no clear holiday standard emerging. Recitations were fairly popular, especially recitations by radio and TV characters. Amos 'n' Andy put out a record of "The Lord's Prayer," which also happened to serve as their TV theme; and Walter Brennan, the veteran character actor who'd become Grandpa on ABC-TV's *The Real*

McCoys, hit in 1962 with "Old Rivers," followed with "Henry Had a Merry Christmas," from the LP *'Twas the Night Before Christmas Back Home.* Several country veterans also yielded LPs, notably *Christmas with Eddy Arnold* and *Christmas Day* by Kitty Wells.

The acts with 1962 pop hits who attempted to cash in on seasonal sales included Bobby Vee, earlier a Buddy Holly emulator, who released "Christmas Vacation"; Elvis imitator Ral Donner, who came up with "(Things That Make Up) Christmas Day"; Detroit's Nathaniel Mayer and the Fabulous Twilights, hot with "Village of Love," a rare Fortune label hit, who brought the same insistent rhythm-and-blues beat to "Mr. Santa Claus"; and the Four Seasons, of "Sherry" fame, who reprised "Santa Claus Is Coming to Town." Two of these acts also issued accompanying LPs: *Merry Christmas from Bobby Vee* and *The Four Seasons' Christmas Greetings.* A third teen throb, albeit one whose star was on the wane, had success with the *Frankie Avalon Christmas Album.*

CHRISTMAS WITH THE MIRACLES

Noel .... Santa Claus Is Coming To Town
I'll Be Home For Christmas ....
White Christmas .... Let It Snow
Silver Bells ...... Winter Wonderland
.... O Holy Night .... Christmas Song
Christmas Everyday

Ten Best Rhythm-and-Blues Christmas Records

1. *Clyde McPhatter and the Drifters, "White Christmas"*

2. *Darlene Love, "Christmas (Baby Please Come Home)"*

3. *Johnny Moore's Three Blazers with Charles Brown, "Merry Christmas, Baby"*

4. *Charles Brown, "Please Come Home for Christmas"*

5. *Mabel Scott, "Boogie Woogie Santa Claus"*

6. Rhythm and Blues Christmas
(A set featuring Chuck Berry, Sonny Til and the Orioles, Baby Washington,
Charles Brown, Clyde McPhatter and the Drifters, the Five Keys,
Lowell Fulson, B. B. King, Marvin and Johnny, and Amos Milburn,
each doing their most memorable Yule material.)

7. *Marvin and Johnny, "It's Christmas"*

8. Charles Brown, Charles Brown Sings Christmas Songs
(Smooth as the Chivas nightcap Santa pours himself as a reward
when he gets back to the Pole.)

9. *Amos Milburn, "Let's Make Christmas Merry Baby"*

10. *Lloyd Glenn, "Sleigh Ride"*

From the novelty file came Bobby (Boris) Pickett, who'd gone to number one at Halloween with "Monster Mash," then actually went top thirty with something called "Monster's Holiday," while Ray Stevens of "Ahab the Arab" fame, another number one, suggested that "Santa Claus Is Watching You." The West Coast duet Jan and Dean, sometimes called the Laurel and Hardy of the surf set, reprised "Frosty the Snow Man" in beachside harmony. The Chipmunks first LP, *Christmas with the Chipmunks,* was also issued in 1962.

Some of the best holiday LPs of the decade found their way into 1962 release. *Merry Christmas, Baby,* the first of the important Christmas anthologies (and maybe the very first Christmas rhythm-and-blues anthology) came out on the Hollywood label in 1962; since then it has found its way into various repackaging schemes on any number of labels. This LP brought about the major early 1960s interest in blues talents like Lowell Fulson and Charles Brown and their songs "Lonesome Christmas" and

"Merry Christmas, Baby," which, in turn, goosed catalog sales of Brown's 1961 hit, "Please Come Home for Christmas."

With the Christmas album a proven market winner, not only major pop labels but even little R&B indies began scouring their artist rosters and the holiday song files (or coming up with variations on traditional themes) for Yule-compatible releases. Ace Records of Jackson, Mississippi, issued Huey "Piano" Smith and the Clowns' *'Twas the Night Before Christmas,* maybe rock and roll's best (and certainly its most raucous) holiday LP, chock-full as it is of New Orleans second-line party vocals. Motown's best Christmas was supplied via the Miracles, whose *Christmas with the Miracles* stayed in print perpetually, as did most of the other Motown holiday releases. Sadly, except for one promo-only single, "Christmas Everyday" by the Miracles, these two albums yielded nary a single 45 release to compete on the end-of-the-year hit parade. Neither did another key R&B release,

Patti LaBelle and the Bluebelles' "Sleigh Bells, Jingle Bells, and Blue Bells," which in 1971 was retitled *Merry Christmas from Patti LaBelle and the Bluebelles.*

Gospel Christmas of 1962 was highlighted by the reissue of Mahalia Jackson's "Silent Night" (reissued again in 1967), and "Joy to the World," along with her LP *Silent Night — Songs for Christmas.* But the Staple Singers also sang about *The 25th Day of December.*

A trio of Christmas record label-switchers presented three pop album efforts: Ferrante and Teicher became United Artists' new piano guys with *Snowbound;* Harry Simeone landed at Decca (which thanks to its association with Bing Crosby could still be considered the semiofficial label of Christmas) with *Joyful Joyful;* and Bing Crosby, after all those years, left Decca for Warner Bros., where one of his first albums was *I Wish You a Merry Christmas,* repackaged as *Bing Crosby's Christmas Classics.*

The year 1963 saw perhaps the most

eclectic batch of Christmas releases of the decade, ranging from the "Wall of Sound" holiday spirit of Phil Spector's album *A Christmas Gift for You* to some of the weirdest novelties from various genres, though it wound up as one of the saddest Christmases in recent recollection.

Frank Sinatra led off the season's nonhit roster by reprising his 1948 "Have Yourself a Merry Little Christmas"; it hadn't hit then either. Also destined to never hit was Rolf Harris's "Six White Boomers," an Australian take on "The Twelve Days of Christmas" by the down-under novelty artist who'd had surprising 1963 success with "Tie Me Kangaroo Down, Sport." Allan Sherman adapted the same theme to "The Twelve Gifts of Christmas," also in 1963, this time done as a farcical commentary on the season's commercialism.

Rockabilly survivor Jack Scott created a dance with a new variation on an old theme, "Jingle Bells Slide." TV personality Soupy Sales spun out odd images in "Santa Claus Is Surfin' to

Town," while real surf rockers the Surfaris added the drum-based sound that made "Wipe Out" a major 1963 hit to their hilarious "The Surfer's Christmas List."

Crooner and militant antirockist Pat Boone had a brief resurgence in 1962 with "Speedy Gonzales," a casual slander of Mexican-Americans, but came no closer to success in 1963 than harmonizing with Beach-Boy-to-be Bruce Johnston on the Beach Boys' sound-alike "Beach Girl." Boone closed out the year with "O Holy Night," a version that attempted vainly to compete with the 1963 rendition by soul giant Jackie Wilson.

Wilson, Brunswick's premier soul artist since leaving Billy Ward and the Dominoes in 1957, and the biggest single influence on everybody at Motown from Smokey Robinson to Michael Jackson, had the spectacular vocal range and willingness to assay straight pop material to make a spectacular Christmas album. Unfortunately, Brunswick continually saddled him with blaring arrangements and weak material, both of which mar his 1963 LP *Merry Christmas from Jackie Wilson.* (Not that that kept it from contemporary chart success or being reissued by Rhino Records in 1991.) The burgeoning sound of soul was further represented by Brook Benton in "You're All I Want for Christmas" and Lloyd Price in "Merry Christmas Mama." Carla Thomas, daughter of Rufus Thomas, answered her own hit "Gee Whiz, Look at His Eyes," the prototypical early example of the Stax-Volt sound, with "Gee Whiz, It's Christmas," along with "All I Want for Christmas Is You" (reissued in 1966). Blues, the secular wing of black America's sorrow songs, nevertheless always came up with a strong Christmas constituency, its needs fulfilled this year by B. B. King's "Christmas Celebration," which was successful enough to be reissued in 1964.

In a sense, Christmas 1963 ended an era — it was the last year in which so many different and variously important pop stars released Christmas records. After the British Invasion landed at the beginning of 1964, the whole music scene turned topsy-turvy, and Christmas records, while still common, no longer seemed an essential part of every hot artist's catalog.

But in 1963, that's exactly what they were. So we got *Christmas with the*

Chipmunks, Vol. 2, which sold so well, even without a new hit, that it was kept in print for several decades. The Osmond Brothers, a sort of live version of the Chipmunks, became a family-oriented subteen sensation after a number of successful appearances on Andy Williams' TV show. *We Wish You a Merry Christmas* was their second LP. Williams himself, now a major turtlenecked TV star whose holiday specials were big hits, ended 1963 with a new version of "White Christmas," from his *Christmas Album* on Columbia. Among other pop giants, Johnny Mathis jumped from Columbia to Mercury for his *Sound of Christmas,* and former Decca artist Harry Simeone joined him in that catalog with *The Wonderful Songs of Christmas.*

Superstars put out Christmas records in those days, although devotees of Roy Orbison still debate whether his version of Willie Nelson's sob story "Pretty Paper" is really a Christmas

record at all. If so, it's certainly the most morbid account of the season since "The Little Match Girl." In any event, the track ranks among the Big O's weaker ballads, although that didn't stop it from going to number fifteen on *Billboard's* Hot 100 chart.

On the other hand, just about every Beach Boys fan loves "Little Saint

Nick," even though that record, issued as a single in 1963 before being compiled on LP the next Yuletide, never cracked the chart. The Beach Boys experienced resistance only in their old neighborhood, because everywhere else they were esteemed as the group that brought Four Freshman–type vocals to the formerly all-instrumental precincts of surf music. But by the time they made "Little Saint Nick," their potent hot-rod harmonies had already become a nationwide sensation. The Beach Boys ranked as the biggest American rock band in the period immediately preceding the advent of the Beatles and their Anglo associates.

But 1963 wasn't dominated by rock band music. At Christmas as throughout the year, a whole assortment of genres and trends appeared. For instance, works by country artists proliferated, among them Johnny Cash's *Christmas Spirit,* Jim Reeves's *Twelve Songs of Christmas,* and Don Reno and Red Smiley's "The True Meaning of Christmas." Also chiming in was Tennessee Ernie Ford, who joined the Roger Wagner Chorale on the *Story of Christmas*.

In fact, you could find Christmas rock records only by looking *hard*. One relatively rare example was "Holiday Hootenanny" by Paul and Paula, a teen appeal Texas duet who'd originally recorded their 1962 number-one hit "Hey, Paula" as Jill and Ray. "Holiday Hootenanny," wrapped into their low-charting (but still charting) *Holiday for Teens* LP, is significant because it tied in to what contemporary music industry observers, even a scant ninety days before the Brits arrived, would have identified as the main youth-music trend of the day: folk music, or at least its self-conscious urban offshoots. Folk enjoyed a major resurgence in 1962 and 1963 via the work of Bob Dylan and Peter, Paul, and Mary. Dylan scooped up the laurels, but on the charts, it was the glossy harmonies of Peter, Paul, and Mary that smoked the competition with

"Puff the Magic Dragon" and remakes of Dylan's "Blowin' in the Wind" and "Don't Think Twice, It's All Right," all of which were top-ten hits. To cap their most successful year, Peter, Paul, and Mary added *A Soulin'* to Christmas of 1963.

If there had been rock critics — or even rock historians — back in 1963, they would have challenged the music biz pundits about the most significant musical trend of the season. Though it seemed unlikely at the time, the most enduring genre that peaked during that year was nothing less than: Girl groups! From the glories of the Crystals and the Ronettes to dozens of little-known and barely remembered wanna-bes, these incandescently romantic records represented the first entry of girls on anything like their own terms into the hallowed halls of rock. And the young women came through at Christmas, too. Little Eva had landed several hits since "The Loco-Motion" topped the charts in 1962, rocking up "Let's Turkey Trot"

and even dueting with Big Dee Irwin on his remake of "Swingin' on a Star." At year's end, she and Irwin featured as a holiday pairing on a new rendition of "The Christmas Song." Songwriter Tony Wine, who composed some memorable if minor tunes for the Phil Spector stable, also worked as an artist in her own write, and for the 1963 Yule season, she contributed an apt "My Boyfriend's Coming Home for Christmas," which summarized a couple of the genre's lyrical and musical clichés. Out of Chicago, the Jaynettes, who had created the busy, mysterious sound of "Sally Go Round the Roses," came up with an equally busy, equally inscrutable holiday concept, "Snowman, Snowman, Sweet Potato Rose."

The Christmas record of 1963 also fit the girl group format. But even though it produced a minor hit in Darlene Love's "Christmas (Baby Please Come Home)," in the year of its release, nobody could have predicted the continuing popularity and long-lived influence exhibited by the Phil Spector–produced album *A Christmas Gift for You from Phil Spector.* Though it charted, *A Christmas Gift for You* hardly turned out to be the capstone to Spector's then-explosive creativity that he clearly intended it to be — except in retrospect. Today, it *is* the one album by which we best remember the producer and writer of "You've Lost That Lovin' Feelin'," "Be

My Baby," "Da Doo Ron Ron," and several dozen other hits. But that Christmas, *A Christmas Gift for You,* like almost every other attempt — musical or otherwise — to spread the glad tidings of the season was swallowed up in the demise of Camelot-on-the-Potomac. For on November 22, 1963, President John F. Kennedy visited Dallas, Texas, and did not return alive. Put simply, once America lost its leader, it was as if it had also lost the taste for Christmas, which made the market for Christmas music, let alone frivolous ol' rock-and-roll Christmas music, worse than thin during the final two months of 1963.

For all intents and purposes, November 22, 1963, could be fixed as the date when holiday music as we had known it since 1942 began to disappear from the scene — for it has taken all the intervening years to begin to sort out what was left of our need to celebrate.

Kennedy's death hardly provided the

only reason for this transformation. It had as much, probably more, to do with the arrival of the Beatles and a host of self-contained, self-consciously hip musical groups no longer dependent upon — or even very interested in — exploring anything so conventional as the traditions and permutations of the Christmas carol. But, foreshadowing as it did the escalating war in Southeast Asia, and the development of the "nonviolent" civil rights movement in Dixie into open racial hostility North as well as South, Kennedy's death provides as perfect a symbol for what changed about American Christmas music as World War II does for the nostalgic longings for the "White Christmas" era.

Phil Spector made it clear that *he* certainly felt that way. And the music of romantic innocence he made his specialty never completely recovered. He would make great records, and huge hits, after 1963, but their tenor would be more adult and soulful. The change can be measured in the differences between "Be My Baby" and "You've Lost That Lovin' Feelin'," or simply by comparing the image of the soft young Ronettes to the rougher, more grown-up Righteous Brothers.

A Christmas Gift for You certainly didn't begin as an elegy. Rather, Spector conceived the album — and this was very much rock and roll's first con-

cept LP — as a celebration both of the sentiment of the season and of his own growing prowess as master of the recording studio.

Spector planned the album — using all the key members of his current artist roster, Love, the Ronettes, the Crystals, and Bob B. Soxx and the Blue Jeans (mainly Bobby Sheen and Darlene Love) — to sing eleven holiday standards plus one original tune, which was

clearly designed to match or even surpass anything in the tradition that extended from "The Twelve Days of Christmas" and "Jingle Bells" to "White Christmas" and "Merry Christmas, Baby." As John J. Fitzpatrick and James E. Fogerty describe it in their 1991 book *Collecting Phil Spector: The Man, the Legend, and the Music,* this would be Christmas music arranged and performed

without concession to traditional interpretation. The recording of each track would receive the care and attention usually reserved for hit singles. . . . In retrospect the project can be viewed as the first rock and roll concept album. The tracks are bound together not only by theme but also by intention of production style, each track emanating from the one before it in a castanet-driven wall of crashing percussion, jangling sleighbells, and perfectly integrated sound effects. The vocalists, to the first-time listener at least, sound as one voice, adding to the uniformity of the sound.

Always obsessive, Spector took himself over the top this time, and brought his cadre of musicians, arrangers, session singers, and even his most indispensable cohort, the veteran engineer Larry Levine, along with him. He checked into the studio in midsummer and didn't emerge until autumn was waning. "Musicians and others participating in those productions unanimously reported the experience as the most grueling of their professional lives," Fitzpatrick and Fogerty contend.

What made Spector's album so revolutionary was the conscious completeness of his achievement. Nothing was left to accident, but the music ranks with the most inspiring he ever produced, and among the most compelling evocations of the holiday spirit ever sung and played. Ronnie Spector reigns triumphant as the queen of Phil's romantic fantasies, singing "Sleigh

Ride." The Crystal's La La Brooks captures an equal mixture of musical majesty and innocence with her opening recitation on "Santa Claus Is Coming to Town," while the Bob B. Soxx tracks amount to a series of brilliant cutting contests between Sheen and Love.

But the most triumphal music on *A Christmas Gift for You* invariably comes on the four great tracks by Darlene

Love. Love gives a special radiance to each of them — the opening "White Christmas," which restores the verse Irving Berlin had cut from the sheet music back in 1942; the tinkly "Marshmallow World"; the surging "Winter Wonderland"; and the album's sole original, "Christmas (Baby Please Come Home)."

Good as she sounds on the standards, on her one try at an original Love proves unsurpassable, turning in perhaps the most shattering Christmas singing ever done. The song's themes recapitulate the grand themes of loneliness, homesickness, and nostalgia associated with Christmas ever since "White Christmas," but when Love drops into her lower register for the opening lines of the chorus, she sounds capable of creating a blizzard all by herself.

A Christmas Gift for You isn't quite a Darlene Love album (although it's as close to a great album as this marvelous singer ever came). But more than any of the other featured performers, it is

Darlene Love who suggests the total passion that the Christmas season is meant to inspire.

The album's conclusion — that bizarrely self-congratulatory recital Spector gives over "Silent Night" — thus qualifies as a massive anticlimax, though some find it honest and moving, not grandiose.

If *A Christmas Gift for You* did not find a wide audience among the record-buying public in 1963, it was widely studied by other musicians and record makers. Significantly, when the Beatles arrived in the United States for the first time the following February, the person preceding them off the plane was none other than Phil Spector. He was returning from a trip to London during which he'd played piano on the first Rolling Stones album. The Beatles would long honor his influence — hiring him to produce their *Let It Be,* reissuing *A Christmas Gift for You* (as *The Phil Spector Christmas Album*) with the imprimatur of their Apple label in 1972, selecting him as the producer

for the early solo works of John Lennon and George Harrison.

The influence of *A Christmas Gift for You* came back home to the States with equal immediacy. You can hear it in the subsequent 1964 Christmas harmonies of two of rock's most-imitated vocal groups, the Beach Boys and the Four Seasons. Although they'd already released their only Christmas LP, when

the Seasons lent their uptown pop treatment to Jimmy Boyd's hit "I Saw Mommy Kissing Santa Claus," it reeked of Bob B. Soxx. And while the Beach Boys had also tried a Christmas release with "Little Saint Nick," their *Christmas Album* (which *was* a commercial hit in 1964, although its only single, "The Man with All the Toys," flopped) is suffused with a Spectorian sensibility, from the way it mixes standards ("We Three Kings of Orient Are") with a cautious amount of original material, to the band tracks (using many of the Wall-of-Sound craftsmen) and even the way that the harmonies are mixed, if not arranged. (Brian Wilson's idea of attractive vocal harmony was always much straighter, less gospel/R&B–derived than Spector's.)

Despite what you may have heard, there *were* other American rock and rollers trying to make tough, serious records in 1964 and 1965. For instance, Minneapolis's manic rockers the Trashmen attempted to follow up the success of their somewhat-plagiarized "Surfin'

Fifteen Hardest-Rocking Christmas Records

1. Bob Seger and the Last Heard,
"Sock It to Me, Santa"

2. Run-DMC, "Christmas in Hollis"

3. Jimi Hendrix,
"The Little Drummer Boy" (EP)

4. Joan Jett and the Blackhearts,
"Little Drummer Boy"

5. The Trashmen, "Dancing with Santa"

6. Ike and Tina Turner,
"Merry Christmas, Baby"

7. Canned Heat and the Chipmunks,
"Christmas Blues"

8. Chuck Berry, "Run Rudolph Run"

9. The Sonics,
"Don't Believe in Christmas"

10. Nathaniel Mayer and the Fabulous
Twilights, "Mr. Santa Claus"

11. Elvis Presley,
"Santa Claus Is Back in Town"

12. Bruce Springsteen,
"Santa Claus Is Coming to Town"

13. The Ravers,
"(It's Gonna Be a) Punk Rock Christmas"

14. Foghat, "Run Run Rudolph"

15. Brenda Lee,
"Rockin' Around the Christmas Tree"

Bird" with "Dancing with Santa" in 1964. It flopped — and they ended up having to pay the Rivingtons for borrowing "Pappa-Oom-Mow-Mow," too. In Texas, a group called the Insight, featuring blues guitarist Johnny Winter and his pianist brother, Edgar, reemphasized the continuing importance of the blues even in the new Anglophile order of things with yet another "Please Come Home for Christmas."

But the bands that most readily picked up on the creative impetus of the British Invasion came from the Seattle/Tacoma Northwest rock-and-roll scene. Chief among them were the Wailers, whose "Tall Cool One" was the coolest instrumental of 1959. A slightly re-vamped version of the same group, which had hit locally with the first white rock "Louie Louie," added a Dylanesque vocal to the sardonic "Christmas Spirit" in 1965. The flip side was by their even more jaundiced little brother band. The Sonics' nasty, nihilistic "Don't Believe in Christmas" was one of a number of sides, including 1964's "The Witch," from that scabrous outfit that helped inspire rock's next great revolt, the seventies punk uprising. In 1965, four tracks each by the Wailers, the Sonics, and the Galaxies, another band of Seattle rockers, were recorded for Etiquette's *Merry Christmas from the Wailers, the Sonics, and the Galaxies.*

Meantime, however, the Beatles and the other English bands that followed them to the States set about revolutionizing the whole of the contemporary popular music scene, Christmas music right along with the rest. So total was their dominance that 1964 and 1965 are among the most checkered and inconsistent years in this whole account, for the new breed of bands displayed far less interest in coping with anybody's list of standard songs or, for that matter, than with honoring any of society's sacred traditions. They were much too busy forging their own songs, sounds, and sensibilities.

The dominant Christmas theme of 1964, the attempt to link the British Invasion with the season, was both its most predictable and, thankfully, also its least successful. Button-down record execs hadn't yet discerned that the new longhair music was a lot more than just another exploitable teenage fad. So there were all manner of attempts at cashing in on the Fab Four's success. Among those that have mercifully never been heard again, except by the bravest record collectors, are the Chipmunks-inspired Three Blonde Mice on "Ringo Bells," Becky Lee Beck's "I Want a Beatle for Christmas," Dora Bryan's "All I Want for Christmas Is a Beatle," Jackie and Jill's "I Want the Beatles for Christmas," and Judy and the Duets' "Christmas with the Beatles."

As for the central instigators of all the furor, though they never recorded a commercial Christmas disc, the Beatles released a year-by-year series of recorded Christmas cards for members of their fan clubs, beginning in 1963 in Great Britain, and in 1964 also offered to U.S. fans. Some of these releases had a party feel; some, recorded with as much professionalism as any of the band's commercial records, were multi-layered playlets in the style of John Lennon's beloved "Goon Show" radio programs; on a few, especially toward the end of the series (which continued through Christmas 1968), they sound as though they're completing a not-especially-welcome chore. All these recordings were collected for reissue on the Beatles' *Christmas Album,* released in 1970, but not yet reissued for the CD age.

The most common refuge for old-guard rockers in search of respite from the uncouth English hordes was Nashville. Brenda Lee had always recorded there, even when she was having hits like "Rockin' Around the Christmas Tree,"

CHILDREN'S CHRISTMAS SONG
TWINKLE TWINKLE LITTLE ME
the S...

but in the mid-sixties she became exclusively identified with country sounds. Her 1964 Christmas record, a remake of Bobby Helms's 1957 hit "Jingle Bell Rock," was followed by the release of her *Merry Christmas* LP. The year's other country Christmas LPs were Jimmie Davis's *It's Christmas Time Again,* Hank Thompson's *Christmas Time,* and

Ernest Tubb's *Blue Christmas,* his first holiday LP, issued fifteen years after the first appearance of its title track. Folkster Burl Ives recorded the hit single "A Holly Jolly Christmas," which he followed with an identically entitled LP in 1965. More firmly country, though still not recorded in Nashville, was Bakersfield hero Buck Owens, whose first Christmas single, the solidly rocking, "I Saw Mommy"–derived "Santa Looked a Lot Like Daddy" also arrived in 1965, as did his first holiday LP, *Christmas with Buck Owens and his Buckaroos.* Jimmy Dean's *Christmas Card,* along with "Bonanza" star Lorne Green's *Have a Happy Holiday* and *Christmas with Jimmie Rodgers,* rounded out this country holiday.

Black music was much less affected by the British Invasion — at least for the first couple of years. By 1964 the Drifters had twice been completely replaced and reshuffled. The group's latest configuration brought back an important former lead vocalist, Johnny

Moore, who had replaced Clyde McPhatter when he got drafted in 1955. Moore took the lead on the group's remake of Nat Cole's "The Christmas Song," backed with "I Remember Christmas," the most memorable original R&B song of that Yule season. Meantime, two of soul's greatest female vocalists both recorded holiday standards in 1964. Before her great soul years at Atlantic, vocalist Aretha Franklin seemed subject to a scheme by Columbia Records' funkless A&R staff to keep her as far as possible from the church or soul music. So she was given a pop arrangement to "Winter Wonderland," although in her predictably singular fashion, Aretha managed to sneak in a few allusions to gospel whoops and moans — and of course, she sang that straight pop as beautifully as anyone of her generation. That same year, Tina Turner, then the female partner (that is, musical chattel) in Ike and Tina Turner, recorded a manic remake of Charles Brown's "Merry Christmas Baby." Two of Franklin and Turner's great influences also caught the Christmas spirit. Jazz vocalist Ella Fitzgerald issued *Sing We Now of Christmas,* while Apollo Records issued *Christmas with Mahalia Jackson,* a collection of her great early 1950s releases, designed to compete with her current Columbia catalog.

The majority of the decade's pop singers attempted to carry on as if no truly great or long-lasting changes had occurred. In 1964 Pittsburgh popster Bobby Vinton, recently hot with the sob-song melodramas "Blue Velvet" and "There, I've Said It Again," recorded "The Bell That Couldn't Jingle" (which was reprised by Herb Alpert in 1970). Vinton followed with the successful LP *A Very Merry Christmas.* Al Martino, a Philadelphia bel canto crooner who first charted in 1952, came up with his second major hit, "I Love You Because," in 1963, which made him sufficiently popular to justify finishing 1964 with "Silver Bells" and the LP *A Merry Christmas,* at least in the eyes of those at Capitol Records who were sure the Beatles couldn't continue inflating profits for long.

In fact, a typical response of the record industry to the British Invasion was an upsurge in the number of straight pop Christmas records issued, as if to capitalize on an anti-Beatles backlash that materialized only in the media, never in the record stores. Among the middle-of-the-road-sters who found themselves making new Christmas records in 1964 were the trio of Bing Crosby, Frank Sinatra, and Fred Waring, who combined for *The Twelve Days of Christmas.* That same year, Peggy Lee released *Christmas Carousel,* Jerry Vale charted with *Christmas Greetings,* and vocalist Jack Jones issued his *Christmas*

Album. In 1965, Crosby returned on his own with *How Lovely Is Christmas* on the children's-oriented Golden label, perhaps a sign that the musical universe was even less stable than previously supposed. Also checking in were has-been pop idol Eddie Fisher with the self-consciously entitled *Mary Christmas* and Peggy Lee, whose *Happy Holiday* cropped up on Capitol. Among 1965's other releases were Percy Faith's *Music of Christmas, Vol. 2,* Andy Williams's "Do You Hear What I Hear" from 1963's *Merry Christmas,* and *Christmas with Patti Page,* including her remake of "Happy Birthday Jesus," all for Columbia, the same label that gave us Little Cindy's original in 1958. Such were the symptoms that showed that the beat revolution's time had come.

Pop instrumentalists also proliferated. In 1964, Ace Cannon, the creator of the 1961 instrumental "Tuff," which was based loosely on a Bill Justis riff, returned with "Blue Christmas," taken from the LP *Christmas Cheers.* Jazz

organist Jimmy Smith, likely inspired by the 1963 release by his rival Jimmy McGriff, charted with *Christmas '64,* and Ramsey Lewis released another holiday hit, *The Sounds of Christmas.* In 1965, the Seattle-based drum-and-guitar instrumental group (not-quite-rock band) the Ventures released the 45

"Sleigh Ride," along with *The Ventures Christmas Album.* The same year, two pop-jazz efforts were attempted, organ grinder Earl Grant's *Winter Wonderland* and faux-Dixieland trumpeter Al Hirt's *The Sound of Christmas.* More authentic jazz emitted from Don Patterson's *Christmas Soul* and Jimmy Smith's follow-up, *Christmas Cookin'.*

Certainly, the American musical enterprise *least* affected by the arrival of the Brits was Motown. By 1965, Berry Gordy, Jr.'s company was America's most successful black business of all time, and the Supremes were, finally, supreme. Gordy certainly hadn't started his company to defy tradition and convention, so one of the trio's first moves during its run at the top of the heap was to make a treacly Christmas 45: "Twinkle Twinkle Little Me" backed with "Children's Christmas Song." Both sides appeared on the trio's *Merry Christmas* LP, a work that stayed in print for several decades, though with much less impact than later

Motown Christmas ditties like Stevie Wonder's "One Little Christmas Tree" and Smokey Robinson's "Bring the Torch Jeannette Isabella/Deck the Halls."

Before he ever thought about meeting Cher, Salvatore Bono, who went on to become not only her husband and partner but a frequent player in Spector's Wall of Sound Orchestra, served as a jack-of-all-trades around Specialty Records, the largest independent record label in Los Angeles, home to Little Richard and beaucoups gospel acts. But although the best of his Specialty releases as an artist sold very few copies indeed, the future Republican mayor of Palm Springs, California, was not necessarily master of none for he penned the excellent screamer "Ko Ko Joe" for Don and Dewey. In 1965, when the Sonny and Cher hit string started, Specialty released an early Bono-led recording called "Comin' Down the Chimney." The label copy credited "Sonny Bono with Little Tootsie."

As for the real Little Tootsie, Cher had no Christmas records in 1965 — or any other year. She did, however, appear as a backup singer on *A Christmas Gift for You,* where Phil Spector used her deep contralto as a kind of human bassoon. See how far ahead of its time that album was?

Chapter Five

SANTA'S GOT A BRAND NEW BAG

The Soul Sixties

AFTER THE British Invasion, the music itself changed almost immediately, with consequences so far-reaching that we're essentially still living in their aftermath. If all Christmas music can be divided into the period before Berlin gave Crosby "White Christmas" and the period after, all of popular music to this very day can basically be divided into the periods before and after the Beatles and their brethren reached the States.

Patterns of buying and, especially, selling music changed much more slowly, but no less permanently. Even through the time of concept albums, pastoral hippie dreams, rock operas, and acid-rock psychedelia, record companies just kept on keeping on, in an effort to stabilize the markets they understood and to exploit, sometimes desperately, the ones they didn't. So the late sixties witnessed a rash of major-star holiday releases of all kinds, even though the developments of that period made the music business much less season-

ally driven and, therefore, by the eighties and nineties, far less dependent on Christmas music.

The flow of Christmas albums never quite ceased. Still, none of the major British acts — not the Stones or the Animals, the Yardbirds or Manfred Mann, the Kinks or the Who — recorded Christmas records. If that was what you wanted, you either had to settle for the Beatles' annual fan club release or turn to a single,

TEN BEST CHRISTMAS SOUL RECORDS

1. *James Brown, "Santa Claus Go Straight to the Ghetto"*

2. *Otis Redding, "Merry Christmas, Baby"*

3. *Donny Hathaway, "This Christmas"*

4. *Hank Ballard and the Midnighters, "Santa Claus Is Coming"*
(Important note: not ". . . Coming to Town, just ". . . Is Coming.")

5. *Clarence Carter, "Back Door Santa"*

6. *The Miracles, "Christmas Everyday"*

7. *Stevie Wonder, "Someday at Christmas"*

8. *Booker T. and the MGs, "Silver Bells"*

9. *James Brown, "Let's Make This Christmas Mean Something This Year"*

10. *Jerry Butler, "O Holy Night"*

somewhat mocking track called "Christmas" from the Who's rock opera *Tommy*. But of carols, Santa, little baby Jesus (*definitely* smaller than the Beatles), Frosty, Rudolph, and warm fireside reminiscences, the new rockers admitted no knowledge. Rock was in the midst of a yearning to be taken seriously, and the domestic joys and hearty frivolities of holiday music would have undercut that seriousness.

The result was a new brand of music biz tumult. If nothing else, the post-Beatles record industry understood that albums could be important profit centers. This benefited many kinds of music that hadn't yet had the opportunity to stretch out, especially soul music. And soul artists still made Christmas records fairly commonly, because soul had been much less affected than rock by the bohemian antitraditionalism that accompanied the new music scene. But what kicked off the soul Christmas-album trend was an album by another kind of genuine musical revolutionary

— that Che Guevara of rhythm, James Brown. *James Brown Sings Christmas Songs* came out in 1966. Accompanying the King Records LP was a pair of singles, Brown's remake of Nat King Cole's "Christmas Song" and his own "Sweet Little Baby Boy." As the King of Soul who had transformed its basic beat with "Papa's Got a Brand New Bag" and "Cold Sweat," James

Brown, and only James Brown, could command the airplay — and sales — for this much product. Brown now began to release at least one Christmas single annually. The best of them was probably the 1967 choice, "Let's Make This Christmas Mean Something This Year," which combined season's greetings, a funky beat, and a marvelously hokey spoken homily about the joys of Christmas Past.

It was the beginning of a virtual flood of soulful late sixties Yule releases. Solomon Burke made his first record, "Christmas Presents," as a child star in 1955, and then was silent for every holiday until 1966, when he dropped the song's titular mirror image, "Presents for Christmas," down appropriately funky chimneys. From Memphis's Stax label came *In the Christmas Spirit*, the companion LP to Booker T. and the MGs' 1965 hit, an arrangement of "Jingle Bells" that placed the emphasis on Steve Cropper's guitar. Released on Stax in 1966, it reappeared on Atlantic in 1969. Atlantic also distributed Dial, for whom the veteran soul shouter — and original rapper — Joe Tex recorded the testifying "I'll Make Everyday Christmas" in 1967. Mainstream jazz artists also found inspiration in the soul explosion; witness guitarist Kenny Burrell's *Have Yourself a Soulful Christmas*, a Cadet album from 1966.

The peak season for soul Santas probably occurred in 1968. That was the year James Brown's "Santa Claus Go Straight to the Ghetto," combined with the more subdued "Let's Unite the World at Christmas," *and* Brown's second Yule LP, *Soulful Christmas*, all came out. Less prolific come 1969, Brown still managed one single, "It's Christmas Time."

Brown's prime Christmas competitor

in the soul market came in the shape of *Soul Christmas,* the superstar

ensemble set released by the Atlantic subsidiary Atco. *Soul Christmas* featured all manner of down-home goodies from the Atlantic and Stax/Volt artist rosters. The range extended from Clarence Carter's crackling, ribald blues, "Back Door Santa," to King Cur-

tis's mellow sax-instrumental remake of "What Are You Doing New Year's Eve," and the lineup included Booker T. and the MGs, Joe Tex, Otis Redding, and Solomon Burke. The collection remains very much in print, with some new tracks, to this day. By decade's end, soul power had given way to black power even in the mid-South, receiving an odd holiday manifestation in the Emotions' "Black Christmas," issued on Volt shortly after the acrimonious dissolution of Stax/Volt's ties to Atlantic, which as a Christmas gift to itself claimed title to virtually all the material the Memphis funkateers had produced over the preceding ten years.

Motown stood slightly outside the soul scene. Although its acts relied just as heavily upon a base in the black community for concert dates on the chitlins circuit, Motown's records consistently aimed for top-forty pop airplay. That didn't mean they were any less soulful; they had merely per-

fected their aim so that it struck a much broader swatch of listeners. Partly, the Gordy group's producers and performers did so by being absolutely shameless in their use of corny material — never more

so than on Stevie Wonder's 1966 "Someday at Christmas." This teary tale of a little pine that so badly wants to be

Ten Best Risqué Christmas Records

Let's say you're giving (or are invited to) a Christmas party and a stripper
is hiding behind the tree, suggestively draped in red and white.
What are the best songs for this affair?
You just want to hear some good old ribald Christmas songs.
What radio station should you tune in?

Our best guess would be the Dr. Demento Show, one or two shows just before
Christmas, or your local alternative rock or public radio station if you pester them
often enough with requests for these titles, stripper not included.

1. Ben Light and His Surf Club Boys,
"Christmas Balls"

2. Ella Fitzgerald,
"Santa Claus Got Stuck in My Chimney"

3. Eartha Kitt, "Santa Baby"

4. Clarence Carter, "Back Door Santa"

5. Jimmy Butler, "Trim Your Tree"

6. Pearl Bailey, "Five Pound Box of Money"

7. Elvis Presley,
"Santa Claus Is Back in Town"

8. Mabel Scott,
"Boogie Woogie Santa Claus"

9. Charles Brown, "Merry Christmas, Baby"

10. Madonna, "Santa Baby"

part of the holiday festivities that an angel grants it the ability to "light up the world" spawned an album of the same name in 1967. Stevie put it over with such potent conviction in its sappy yet compelling sentimentality that it's remained in print for a quarter century, a rare feat for *any* pop album.

The Supremes and the Miracles had made Christmas albums in the early sixties, as the Motown aesthetic was just developing. The Temptations became the fourth of the company's superstars to record a Christmas disc, on a 45 that paired "Rudolph the Red-Nosed Reindeer" with "Silent Night" in 1968, followed by their Christmas album, *The Temptations' Christmas Card,* in 1969. That was all from them until 1982, when a re-formed version of the group re-recorded "Silent Night." Several other key Motown acts — most surprisingly Marvin Gaye, but also Martha and the Vandellas and sax honker Jr. Walker — never did get to make Christmas records.

With the biggest white rock stars,

from the Brits abroad to Dylan and the Byrds back home, opting out of the Christmas sweepstakes, fans of new Yule fodder had slim pickings. Christmas novelty tunes had all but disappeared, though Freddy Cannon was heard on one pseudonymously, the small-selling "Santa's Little Helper" by the Pipsqueeks on Warner Bros. in 1966. Not exactly a novelty (but what else could you call it, a

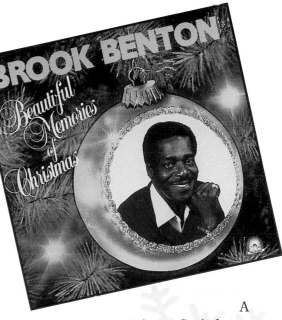

commercial suicide pact?) was the absolutely bizarre 1968 duet pairing of Canned Heat with the Chipmunks. "Christmas Blues" and its flip side, "The Chipmunk Song," created a sound that not even the most diehard fans of Canned Heat's boogie could accept and anybody still naive enough to be a fan of the Chipmunks just wouldn't get. But both groups recorded for Liberty Records, which desperately wanted to make sense — money — out of what had happened on the hip music scene.

The end result could be termed Christmas music's first mule.

Pop-folk fans could choose between the Brothers Four's *Merry Christmas* or the Lettermen's *For Christmas This Year,* both of which came out in 1966. For the real mood music fan, the same season brought Wayne Newton's *Songs for a Merry Christmas.* Both the Lettermen and Newton recorded for Capitol, and both sold plenty of records, even as the new rock ideal was taking over.

A future Capitol star, Michigan rocker Bob Seger, recorded "Sock It to Me Santa," with his band, the Last Heard, for the local Hideout label, although the master ultimately wound up with Philadelphia's Cameo label in 1966. Seger sang like a white boy who'd had a huge hunk of funk dropped into his stocking, making the gospel-bred title phrase into a hook

Aretha Franklin would hammer home the next year in her number-one hit "Respect." Seger's "Sock It to Me" ranks with the best of an early career that climaxed with "Ramblin' Gamblin' Man" in 1968.

The sixties' final significant pseudonymous release was "Christmas Is My Time of Year," the highly regarded single by Christmas Spirit — in reality a pretty fair joint venture between Linda Ronstadt and the Turtles, working up a 1968 California Christmas sound for the Turtles' White Whale label. Ronstadt hadn't yet had her first hit — the previous year's "A Different Drum" had been credited to a group called the Stone Poneys — while the Turtles had pretty much peaked after "Elenore" made the top ten in October (their hip credentials dampened by an appearance at Lyndon Johnson's White House during the height of antiwar sentiment). But here the group — principally Howard Kaylan and Mark Volman, known in the seventies and eighties as Flo and Eddie — joined Ronstadt in virtually timeless sweet harmony, a fine conclusion to what had been, even during its seasons of joy, a most turbulent decade.

Chapter Six

PLEASE COME HOME FOR CHRISTMAS

Corporate Rock's Holiday Bonus

*T*HE 1970s represented a time of tremendous musical expansion, as hard rock solidified into heavy metal, pop became dominated by a new breed called singer-songwriters, sixties superstars aged into either early retirement or dependable perennial multiplatinum award-winners, and soul splintered into funk, disco, and half a dozen other fragments. The Christmas season became progressively less important;

although it was still the most lucrative time of year to release a star's album, records now began to be marketed on more of a year-round basis. And with everybody — rockers, soft and hard, funkateers, discolettes — insisting on using their songs as vehicles for personal intimacies and expressive, often exhibitionist, individualism, the community of good cheer and warm family feeling that Christmas songs evoked came to seem more and more anachronistic. The reality wasn't just the drying up of the previous era's annual flood of seasonal novelty discs. It was the labeling of *all* new Christmas records as a species of novelty, rather than a staple of the trade.

Other factors also intruded. Pop music had become a battleground in the beginning stages of the cultural civil war that racked America for the remainder of the decade. For black artists, among the very few public spokesmen for a community under continuous economic and social duress, the pressure was even more intense.

Twenty Most Valuable Christmas Records

1. The Moonglows, "Hey Santa Claus," 1953, $800.
(Flip side, "Just a Lonely Christmas," a ballad, is the perfect alternative to the jump "Hey Santa Claus." Don't pay more than five bucks for the red vinyl 45; it's a bootleg.)

2. The Five Keys, "It's Christmastime," 1951, $750.

3. Elvis Presley, "Blue Christmas," RCA Victor 0808, promo 45, 1957, $750.
(The 1964 reissue, RCA Victor 0720, with picture sleeve, is valued at $50.)

4. The Orioles, "Lonely Christmas," Jubilee 5017, 45 rpm, 1950, $500.
(Jubilee 5001 from 1949 was issued only on 78 rpm, $30.)

5. Elvis Presley Christmas Album, 1957, $500.

6. The Hepsters, "Rockin' 'N' Rollin' with Santa Claus," 1955, $400.

7. The Ebonaires, "Love for Christmas," 1955, $300.

8. The Beatles, "The Beatles' Christmas Record," UK-only release, flexi-disk, 1963, $250.

9. The Sabres, "Cool Cool Christmas," 1955, $250.

10. The Beatles, "Season's Greetings from the Beatles," 1964, $200.
(Released in UK as "Another Beatles' Christmas Record.")

11. The Coolbreezers, "Let Christmas Ring," 1958, $150.

12. The Beatles, "The Beatles' Third Christmas Record," 1965, $125.
(Released by Beatles USA Limited Fan Club.)

13. The Beatles, "Everywhere It's Christmas" (vinyl-coated postcard), 1966, $125.

14. The Beatles, "Christmastime (Is Here Again)," 1967, $125.

15. The Beatles, "The Beatles' Christmas Album," 1970, $100.

16. The Voices, "Santa Claus Boogie," "Santa Claus Baby," 1955, $80.

17. The Beatles, "The Beatles' 1968 Christmas Record" (7-inch flexi disc), 1968, $80.

18. "A Christmas Gift for You from Phil Spector," 1963, $80 (original Philles pressing only)

19. The Beatles, "Happy Christmas 1969," 1969, $60.

20. Johnny Moore's Three Blazers, "Merry Christmas, Baby," Swing Time 238, 45 rpm, 1950, $50.
(Original issued only on 78 rpm.)

Price estimates are our best guesses as of Christmas 1992.

So by 1970, James Brown couldn't avoid politics if he wanted to (and he didn't) even at Christmas, and he came up with both a single and an LP called *Hey America* to express his seasonal sentiments. Brown added his final Christmas single (for a long while, at least) entitled "Santa Claus Is Definitely Here to Stay," proving he's a man of many moods, even in a single season. In the late eighties, Rhino Records combined much of Brown's best Christmas material for the compact disc *Santa's Got a Brand New Bag.*

Always more cautious and conservative — if not necessarily any less "black" — Motown turned its newest number-one hitmakers, the Jackson Five, toward more traditional Yule numbers. The J5's importance is twofold: In Michael Jackson, the group introduced the most important new vocalist of the era; and the group performed material that saw the world not just from a teen or preteen viewpoint but from a *black* kid's perspective. This was true even when they adapted material from the 1950s, like "Santa Claus Is Coming to Town." They maintained the essential innocence of the message in their *Christmas Album,* but without sacrificing any of their credibility, which played a key role in making them Motown's final and biggest star-making success story.

Nineteen seventy also saw the initial release of Donny Hathaway's fine "This Christmas." The song's fusion of holiday imagery — everything *but* chestnuts roasting on an open fire — and promissory romance made it a throwback to "The Christmas Song" and "Merry Christmas Baby." And Hathaway, who sounded so much like Stevie Wonder he was often mistaken for him on the radio, put the tune over with a compelling combination of innocence and assurance. Yet the turbulent arranger for Aretha Franklin and Roberta Flack never had a big hit with the song; it didn't even hit the *Billboard* Christmas chart until 1972. Nevertheless, "This Christmas" was perhaps the most influential Christmas song of the seventies. For the next twenty years, balladeers from Luther Vandross to Alexander O'Neal would try to match Hathaway. Many did good jobs, but none came close to topping him.

Otherwise, R&B and its related genres produced very little Christmas music in the seventies.

Probably the most notable releases were the two Latin-disco instrumental albums by the Salsoul Orchestra,

both of which charted but neither of which offered anything but barely serviceable aural wallpaper with a seasonal motif.

When is a Christmas release not a Christmas release? Mainly when it's "Santa Dog" by the Residents, an avant-garde group specializing in the outer reaches of sonic listenability. Its creators issued the disc on their own Ralph label in 1972. Typically, the song has no discernible lyrical connection to the holiday at hand. Also landing from territory located somewhere between outer space and left field was "Santa Claus and His Old Lady" by Cheech and Chong, a song that helped bring the comedy duo's cannabis-based humor to a high that lasted from 1971 through 1973, the years their doped-out "Whuzzup, Santa?" skit stayed on the market.

The year 1971 brought producer Phil Spector back to Christmas for the first time since his 1963 album *A Christmas Gift for You*. After John Lennon reconciled himself to the Beatles' demise, he latched on to Spector as the perfect production partner for himself and his wife/collaborator, Yoko Ono. They immediately concocted a number-three hit, "Instant Karma (We All Shine On)," and went on to make several albums together, including the revelatory *John Lennon / Plastic Ono Band* and the ground-breaking *Imagine.* (Spector had been reclusive for years after his heralded attempt to build a Wall of Sound around Tina Turner with Ike and Tina's "River Deep Mountain High" collapsed at the box office.) At the end of 1971, just after *Imagine,* they teamed up for "Happy Xmas (War Is Over)," a melody some say is based on the folk standard "Stewball," but which, writer Richard Williams reports, Spector alleged, during the session, Lennon had pinched from Spector's own 1958 production of the Paris Sisters' "I Love How You Love Me." Only a hipster with the impregnable credentials of John Ono Lennon, as the label copy called him, could have used a *Christmas* song, and a sentimental one to boot, to follow up one of the most shattering personal statements ever placed on LP.

Lennon's buddy Elton John put out "Step into Christmas" on MCA in 1973, with the bizarrely entitled "Ho Ho Ho, Who'd Be a Turkey at Christmas" as its flip. Stevie Wonder finished out the year 1972 with "What Christmas Means to Me." Flying high with a series of the most thoroughly composed R&B albums ever made, Wonder also appeared on *The Motown Christmas Album,* which featured Diana Ross and the Supremes, Smokey Robinson and the Miracles, the Temptations, the Jackson Five, and Michael Jackson, too. But the rest of the mid-seventies — straight through to 1977, when a *lot* of things began to change — saw scant Christmas releases, certainly nothing that made an impact. The one famous Christmas track recorded during this period was Bruce Springsteen's live (at C. W. Post College on Long Island) "Santa Claus Is Coming to Town."

Although it was issued to selected radio stations just after he set it down in 1975, and even though Springsteen and the E Street Band continued to perform their raucous adaptation of Phil Spector's arrangement for the Crystals onstage for the next decade, the track didn't reach vinyl until 1985.

The oldies-based *Soulful Christmas* featured Brook Benton, Jerry Butler, Charles Brown, Patti LaBelle, and Sonny Til and the Orioles doing vintage material, but all the tracks were 1977 remakes. Nevertheless, the LP, which even borrowed its title from the late sixties, stayed in print until the 1980s. The same year, the Kinks, who had never cut a Christmas track in their British Invasion heyday, finally succumbed to leader Ray Davies' penchant for sentimentality and issued "Father Christmas" on both seven-inch and twelve-inch singles (one of the first Christmas examples of this common practice of the late 1970s and 1980s). "Father

Christmas," you may not know, is what Brits call Santa Claus. From the same period, Greg Lake of Emerson, Lake, and Palmer

put out a solo Christmas ditty, his "I Believe in Father Christmas," which was less bombastic and more heartfelt than his band's everyday fare.

In 1977 the rock culture that had

developed since the Beatles exploded once again. In part, this came about because of fragmentation and stagnation within that culture; the best-selling bands of the sixties and early seventies had, for the most part, combined to form a relatively risk-free series of commercial enterprises that had lost most connection to what was really meaningful or exciting. There was also an element of despair involved, as the world economy set into a long, slow decline after the rampant prosperity of the post–World War II period. But in another way, the new rebellion — which centered on a stripped-down, vulgar, crude form of rock dubbed "punk" — was just a new group of kids' chance to differentiate themselves from their moms, pops, and older brothers and sisters by inventing sounds the old farts couldn't stand to be in the same room with. Thus, in 1977, a studio group called the Ravers gave birth to the calculated "(It's Gonna Be a) Punk Rock Christmas," punk's first nod to the season. Some of

the lyrics were derivative, especially of the Crossfires' "Surfer's Christmas List," which provided the idea for the punk rocker's Santa wish list in the lyrics (among the wishes was one for ten thousand records by the English garage punks Eddie and the Hot Rods).

As always, the music industry responded slowly to changes in the music scene. For the most part, it felt bathed in prosperity during those days in the late seventies. It wasn't until the tag end of the eighties that such practices as rampant overshipping of unsalable merchandise caught up with, and nearly bankrupted, many labels. Still, the corporations now had what they apparently wanted — a star-driven business with a cadre of superstars fairly guaranteed to sell millions of units of whatever they chose to put out.

Few chose to put out Christmas records. In 1978 the soft-rock Eagles decided to take a new peek at Charles

Brown's "Please Come Home for Christmas." Their new rendition, an early example of Eagles vocalist Don Henley's affinity for blues singing, charted in the top twenty. It was the first big-league Christmas hit since Lennon's in 1971. Another 1978 superstar remake came from Rolling Stones guitarist Keith Richards, who selected

for his first-ever solo foray the 1959 hit "Run Rudolph Run," by his maximum hero, Chuck Berry.

Even harder rock came in promo-only form (meaning it was ubiquitous at FM "album rock" radio but couldn't be purchased by consumers) in 1979, when somebody unearthed a tape of "The Little Drummer Boy" by, of all the unlikely actors in the psychedelic universe, the Jimi Hendrix Experience. This instant collector's item had been recorded in 1969, two years before Jimi's death, when Hendrix, Billy Cox, and Buddy Miles were warming up before a session at the Record Plant in New York. Jimi broke into the song spontaneously, according to the liner notes; then "Billy and Buddy promptly jumped in to accompany Jimi and the holiday spirit took over." The EP also contained rocked-up renditions of "Silent Night" and "Auld Lang Syne." But the really important track was "The Little Drummer Boy," which sparked several other hard-rocking versions of Harry Simeone's greatest hit, notably Joan Jett's ragamuffin take in 1981, and Bob Seger's more bombastic 1987 assault. The Hendrix track wasn't anywhere near as big a hit as the Eagles' or Lennon's had been, but it was the last time an individual hard-rock star would make much of a dent in either airplay or sales with a Christmas disc.

MERRY CHRISTMAS

NJ 497

FROM SANTA AND BRUCE SPRINGSTEEN

If you don't play Bruce's new collectible album "The Wild, The Innocent and the E Street Shuffle," you can cover coal in your stocking for Christmas

Chapter Seven

A Very Special Christmas

Christmas Comes Back

THE START of the 1980s brought perhaps the final Christmas novelty classic, a record that well could become another "Rudolph the Red-Nosed Reindeer" (it's still too early to tell) — though if that is the case, history will have fulfilled the dictum of Karl Marx and repeated itself as farce. That's certainly an apt summation of "Grandma Got Run Over by a Reindeer," an epic that is closer in its overall effect to what Gene Autry must've had in mind when he recorded his last-gasp "Santa's Comin' in a Whirlybird" back in 1959. Credited to Elmo and Patsy, this unlikeliest of all contemporary holiday hits was originally put out in 1979 on the tiny Kim Pat label based in Fayetteville, Tennessee.

The record blended Bob Wills–style roadhouse hollers, a rhythmic style that approaches a degraded brand of rockabilly, and vocals by the semipro (to be generous) duo from Windsor, California. Elmo and Patsy tenderly sang bizarre lyrics about a nonsensical holiday tragedy and a genuinely dysfunctional family's response. The ludicrous scenario was pure Nashville song-factory stuff, peppered with puns and allusions to a clichéd bunch of beer-soaked, greedy relatives. Yet somehow, the song struck a chord with millions. It must be its irreverence about everything from Santa himself (who should have been denied a license because he's "a man who drives a sled and plays with elves") to Grandma (who is missed primarily because her hair rinse would have blended so well with the silver-blue candles) and Grandpa (who takes it well, drinking beer and playing cards with Cousin Mel). A record that sneered at Christmas — like the satires Stan Freberg created in the fifties or the rock-and-roll jeremiads the Wailers and the Sonics spat out in the sixties — had no chance of becoming a hit. But a record that embraced the season's hokiness and sentimentality by taking every element of the ritual to its illogical extreme would be embraced in return. And so the saga began.

By 1982, "Grandma Got Run Over by a Reindeer" had been reissued on

another tiny country-oriented label, Oink (honestly), and re-recorded for a third, Soundwaves. Much of the song's success has to be credited to exposure via radio's "Dr. Demento Show," which has maintained "Grandma Got Run Over by a Reindeer" as a holiday favorite, along with songs by Stan Freberg and Tom Lehrer, for the better part of twenty years. In 1982 an actual Elmo and Patsy *Grandma Got Run Over by a Reindeer* LP came out, followed by the remake on Epic in 1984. How to discern the remake? Epic's version uses piano. One way or another, though, the success of Elmo and Patsy suggests the dire straits Christmas music had fallen into by the early 1980s.

Not that interesting Christmas music didn't sometimes get made — it just had more trouble being widely heard, as the music scene continued to fragment and implode in so many varying patterns. The 1980s began with the first hit Christmas rap record, Kurtis

Blow's "Christmas Rappin'," issued on Mercury in 1981. Hardly a landmark in the history of hip-hop, it was nonetheless a skillfully rhymed account of an Afro (or at least, Afro-American) -centric holiday approach. To date, despite the many black nationalists in the rap scene, there are no significant records celebrating the newly cre-

Twenty Artists We Wish Had Recorded a Christmas Song

1. Sam Cooke
2. Buddy Holly
3. Little Richard
4. Johnny Ace
5. George Clinton
6. The Four Tops
7. Ricky Nelson
8. Wilson Pickett
9. The Spinners
10. The Isley Brothers
11. Gene Pitney
12. Ritchie Valens
13. Dick Dale and the Deltones
14. The Clovers
15. The Righteous Brothers
16. Bo Diddley
17. The Young Rascals
18. Sly and the Family Stone
19. Jr. Walker and the All Stars
20. Mary Wells
(tied with)
Marvin Gaye
(though he did make one
very rare Christmas video)

ated African-American holiday Kwanza, which extends from December 26 to New Year's.

In 1982 Pavillion secured the right to reissue *A Christmas Gift for You* and in order to promote it put out a double-sided single, nineteen years after its initial release, featuring the Ronettes' "I Saw Mommy Kissing Santa Claus" on one side and the Crystals' "Rudolph the Red-Nosed Reindeer" on the flip. Speaking of Rudolph, Dave Edmunds again reprised Chuck Berry's "Run Rudolph Run" for Columbia in 1982, much the same way his fellow Chuck Berry worshipper Keith Richards had brought it back in 1978.

But by now, when seasonal material got recorded, it was likely to use the holidays simply as the token of a broader moral parable, like U2's "New Year's Day" in 1983, or as a mere afterthought, like Prince's B-side "Another Lonely Christmas" from 1984, or Bruce Springsteen's Otis Redding–style "Merry Christmas, Baby," a complement to his

five-LP
live box set in 1986.

More often, the most engrossing holiday listening came from reissues of hits and obscurities from bygone days. Rhino Records, now closely identified as the home of the world's best reissues of Christmas Past, began the trend in 1984 with a matched set, *Rockin' Christmas of the 50s* and *Rockin' Christmas of the 60s,* both containing selections split between hits and fairly arcane novelties and obscurities.

The most important music scene development of 1984 began at Christmas but, once again, transcended the date. That was Band Aid's "Do They Know It's Christmas," a multiact charity single that reached only number thirteen on the charts but initiated both a worldwide relief campaign for the starving millions in Ethiopia and a series of trendy charity concerts for a variety of good causes, first with USA for Africa's "We Are the World" in early 1985 and culminating the following summer with Band Aid's successor, the live (from both Philadelphia and London) satellite-TV concert "Live Aid."

Band Aid began coming together after Bob Geldof, leader of a minor Anglo-Irish band called the Boomtown Rats, saw a television special about the famine caused by the civil war in Ethiopia. He enlisted a friend, Midge Ure, guitarist for the modernesque band Ultravox, and together they wrote "Do They Know It's Christmas?" about starving children in third-world countries. Geldof and Ure then enlisted a number of friends and acquaintances, mostly UK acts like Paul Young, Boy George of Culture Club, Sting, Phil Collins, Duran Duran, Spandau Ballet, Bananarama, and members of U2, Ultravox, Status Quo, and Heaven 17. A couple of members of those ace funkateers Kool

and the
Gang were the only
Yanks aboard. The musical
result was, to use the vernacular, rather
twee. But its impact, on charts and
hearts, proved far more powerful. In
England, where the tradition of seasonal sob stories extends back beyond
Charles Dickens's *A Cricket on the
Hearth* and *A Christmas Carol,* the
record went straight to number one and

became one of the biggest hits of all
time. Although its run in America
turned out to be less promi-
nent, Geldof eventually found
himself dispensing about a hundred million dollars in famine
relief, and dealing with the govern-
ment politicians, officials, and
bureaucrats of three continents.

Moving from the significant to the
sublimely ridiculous, Rhino continued
its Christmas series in 1985 with *Dr.
Demento Presents the Greatest Christmas
Novelty Records of All Time,* which
returned to the fore the Chipmunks,
Spike Jones, Allan Sherman, Gayla
Peevey, Stan Freberg, Tom Lehrer,
the original Elmo and Patsy, Yogi
Yorgesson, Cheech and Chong, and
Weird Al Yankovic, each doing something downright Christmasy, and often
outright weird.

The early '90s have revealed what
may be a return to the pre-1960s trend
of major artists recording substantial
Christmas releases. Country star Randy

Travis released *An Old Time Christmas*
in 1989, and 1992 saw a slew of releases
ranging from heavyweights like Garth
Brooks and Neil Diamond to oddballists
Mojo Nixon and the Toadlickers. At the
same time, record companies' reissues
of backlist Christmas recordings
exploded, as baby boomers looked for
holiday tunes to play on their new CD
players.

The most important
Christmas

Twenty Artists We're Glad Never Recorded a Christmas Song

1. John Belushi	11. Michael Bolton (yet)
2. The Doors	12. Cher
3. George Michael	13. The cast of Hee Haw
4. The Kingsmen	14. Herman's Hermits
5. The Bee Gees	15. The Moody Blues
6. Pink Floyd	16. Helen Reddy
7. The Grateful Dead	17. The Monkees
8. Twisted Sister	18. Alice Cooper
9. Jefferson Airplane	19. Randy Newman
10. Mike Curb	20. The Dave Clark Five

release of recent years combined tradition — both Christmas and rock-and-roll tradition — and charity with results that still reverberate. It was created by producer Jimmy Iovine back in 1987.

Iovine's Christmas associations ran deep; as a young engineer at the Record Plant in the early seventies, he was assigned to assist John Lennon and Phil Spector, fresh off "Happy Xmas (War Is Over)," when they were cutting Lennon's oldies album *Rock and Roll.* In the mid-seventies, Iovine engineered Bruce Springsteen's *Born to Run,* including its most famous outtake, "Santa Claus Is Coming to Town." After also engineering Springsteen's *Darkness on the Edge of Town,* Iovine went on to become one of the premier rock producers of the early eighties, coming up with hits for Patti Smith, Tom Petty and the Heartbreakers, Stevie Nicks, and U2.

All this only served as prologue for Iovine's most famous record, or at least the one that he most dominated personally. It came into being after his father and another close family member died during the 1986 Christmas season. Iovine became convinced that unless he could find a way to redeem it, the end-of-the-year holiday season would bum him out for the rest of his life. His wife, Vicki, suggested making an album in the great tradition of Spector's *A Christmas Gift for You,* using contemporary artists and more up-to-date but still traditional material. She also proposed doing it for the Special Olympics, the athletics event for the disabled closely associated with the Kennedy family. Jimmy and the Kennedys agreed to try, and Iovine spent a year turning his considerable persuasive and production skills to the album that became *A Very Special Christmas,* issued on A&M just in time to indeed redeem Christmas 1987, at least musically.

Those who eventually succumbed to Iovine's relentless blandishments included the Pointer Sisters, the Eurythmics, Whitney Houston, Bruce Springsteen and the E Street Band, the Pretenders, John Cougar Mellencamp, Sting, Madonna, U2, Bob Seger and the Silver Bullet Band, Bryan Adams, Bon Jovi, Alison Moyet, Stevie Nicks, and Run-DMC. The song pairings designedly recapitulated many of Spector's, notably on the opening reprise of Jack Nitzche's "Santa Claus Is Coming to Town" arrangement, with vocals by the Pointers, and Mellencamp's "I Saw Mommy Kissing Santa Claus," which shoots for the same degree of plaintiveness as the Ronettes achieved.

Least successful of all the Spectoresque material is U2's wooden "Christmas (Baby Please Come Home)," proof positive, even though Darlene Love herself took over the backup vocals, that it's a mistake to send a Bono to do a woman's job. Both albums also end with "Silent Night," although Spector's Wall-of-Sound recitative can't match the beauty Stevie Nicks brought to her somber but all-stops-out version.

But what really allowed *A Very Special Christmas* to take on the role for the 1980s that Spector's *A Christmas Gift for You* had provided for the intervening twenty-five years was getting a select few performers to step outside the Christmas genre and make records that spoke eloquently in their own idiom. Chief among these are Run-DMC's joyously raucous rap "Christmas in Hollis," Madonna's smolderingly camp remake of Eartha Kitt's "Santa Baby," Bon Jovi's slavering but somehow still apt "Back Door Santa," and the absolutely timeless carols by Sting (on the recent "Gabriel's Message") and Alison Moyet (on the traditional "Coventry Carol").

Unlike his mentor and role model, Jimmy Iovine never spoke a word on *A*

Very Special Christmas, but then, he didn't need to. He'd left his listeners a perfectly eloquent Christmas message, written indelibly in the grooves, that spoke beautifully of his love for the season and, in keeping with the seasonal sentiment Irving Berlin established almost half a century earlier, his warmly nostalgic memory of family and friends and days gone by. Many others would make Christmas discs in the ensuing years — in 1992, Iovine himself made a second volume for the Special Olympics — but *A Very Special Christmas* was the record they'd be measuring themselves against for a good long time to come. Like all the finest Christmas gifts, it keeps on giving, each time we hear it.

CHRISTMAS EVERY DAY

365 Great Christmas Singles

HERE ARE some of the best, most successful, most bizarre, disturbing, or unexpected Christmas recordings (45 or 78 rpm) from the late 1930s to the early 1990s — 365 of our picks, enough to enjoy a holiday song of your choice for Christmas and every other day of the year as well. Some of these releases can be found on compact disc, but most have been long out of print. So if you see one you like, buy it, quick!

The Ad Libs. "Santa's on His Way" (Johnny Boy 4), 1988.

Gene Ammons. "Boppin' with Santa" (Chess 1445), 1950.

The Andrews Sisters. "Christmas Tree Angel" (Decca 27251), 1950.

Paul Anka. "I Saw Mommy Kissing Santa Claus" (ABC/Paramount 10163), 1960.

Argent. "Christmas for the Free" (Epic 10972), 1972.

Louis Armstrong. "Cool Yule" (Decca 28943), 1953.

———. "Christmas Night in Harlem" (Decca 29710), 1955.

Eddy Arnold. "C-H-R-I-S-T-M-A-S" (RCA Victor 0124), 1949.

Chet Atkins. "Jingle Bells" (RCA Victor 6314), 1955.

Gene Autry. "Here Comes Santa Claus" (Columbia 37942), 1947; (Columbia 20377), 1948, 1953; (Columbia Hall of Fame 33165), 1970.

———. "Rudolph the Red-Nosed Reindeer" (Columbia 38610), 1949; (Columbia Hall of Fame 50075), 1955; (Columbia Hall of Fame 33165), 1970.

———. "Frosty the Snow Man" (Columbia 38907), 1950–1953; (Columbia Hall of Fame 50075), 1955.

———. "Santa's Comin' in a Whirlybird" (Republic 2002), 1959.

Gene Autry and Rosemary Clooney. "The Night Before Christmas Song" (Columbia 39876), 1952.

♪♪ 87

Jim Backus. "I Was a Teenage Reindeer" (Dice 101), 1959.

Ross Bagdasarian. "Let's Have a Merry Merry Christmas" (Mercury 70254), 1953.

Pearl Bailey. "Five-Pound Box of Money" (Roulette 4206), 1959.

Hank Ballard and the Midnighters. "Santa Claus Is Coming" (King 5729), 1962.

Band Aid. "Do They Know It's Christmas" (Columbia 04749), 1984.

The Beach Boys. "Little Saint Nick" (Capitol 5096), 1963.

———. "The Man with All the Toys" (Capitol 5312), 1964.

Harry Belafonte. "Mary's Boy Child" (RCA Victor 6735), 1956; (RCA Gold Standard 0323), 1957.

Jesse Belvin. "I Want You with Me Xmas" (Modern 1006), 1956.

Brook Benton. "This Time of the Year" (Mercury 71554), 1959; (Mercury 71730), 1960; (Mercury Celebrity 30101), 1961; (Mercury 72214), 1963.

Chuck Berry. "Merry Christmas Baby" (Chess 1714), 1959.

———. "Run Rudolph Run" (Chess 1714), 1959.

Elvin Bishop. "Silent Night" (Capricorn 0248), 1975.

Mel Blanc. "I Tan't Wait till Quithmuth" (Capitol 1853), 1951; (Capitol 2169), 1952; (Capitol 2619), 1953; (Capitol 3191), 1954.

Kurtis Blow. "Christmas Rappin'" (Mercury 4009), 1981; (Mercury 12″ 41009), 1981.

The Blue Notes. "O Holy Night" (Val-ue 215), 1960.

The Blues Magoos. "Santa Claus Is Coming to Town" (Mercury 72762), 1967.

Johnny Bond. "Jingle Bells Boogie" (Columbia 20756), 1950.

Gary U.S. Bonds. "Call Me for Christmas" (Legrand 1045), 1965.

Boney M. "Mary's Boy Child" (Hansa Sire 1036), 1978.

Sonny Bono with Little Tootsie. "Comin' Down the Chimney" (Specialty 733), 1965.

Booker T. and the MGs. "Jingle Bells" (Stax 203), 1966.

Pat Boone. "O Holy Night" (Dot 16547), 1963.

David Bowie and Bing Crosby. "The Little Drummer Boy" (RCA 13400), 1982.

Jimmy Boyd. "I Saw Mommy Kissing Santa Claus" (Columbia 39871), 1952; (Columbia 40070), 1953; (Columbia Hall of Fame 50078), 1955.

Happy Holidays to all...

——. "Reindeer Rock" (Columbia 40601), 1955.

The Brady Bunch. "Silver Bells" (Paramount 0062), 1970.

Charles Brown. "Merry Christmas, Baby" (Aladdin 3348), 1956; (Imperial 5902), 1962–1965; (Liberty 5902), 1970; (United Artists 582), 1974; (Liberty 1393), 1980.

——. "Please Come Home for Christmas" (King 5405), 1961.

James Brown. "Let's Make This Christmas Mean Something This Year" (King 6072), 1967.

——. "Santa Claus Go Straight to the Ghetto" (King 6203), 1968; (Polydor 14162), 1972.

Buchanan and Goodman. "Santa and the Satellite" (Luniverse 107), 1957.

Solomon Burke. "Christmas Presents" (Apollo 485), 1955.

——. "Presents for Christmas" (Atlantic 2369), 1966.

Jerry Butler. "O Holy Night" (Vee Jay 371), 1961.

Jimmy Butler. "Trim Your Tree" (Gem 222), 1953.

Edd Byrnes. "Yulesville" (Warner Bros. 5121), 1959.

The Cadillacs. "Rudolph the Red-Nosed Reindeer" (Josie 807), 1956.

The Cameos. "Merry Christmas" (Cameo 123), 1957.

Eddie C. Campbell. "Santa's Messin' with the Kid" (Rooster Blues 46), 1977.

Canned Heat and the Chipmunks. "Christmas Blues" (Liberty 56079), 1968.

Ace Cannon. "Blue Christmas" (Hi 2084), 1964.

Art Carney. "Santa and the Doodle-Li-Boop" (Columbia 40400), 1954.

The Carpenters. "Merry Christmas Darling" (A&M 1236), 1970–1973; (A&M 1648), 1974–1976; (A&M 1991), 1977; (A&M 8620), 1979.

Clarence Carter. "Back Door Santa" (Atlantic 2576), 1968.

Wilf Carter. "The Night Before Christmas in Texas" (RCA Victor 0292), 1951.

Johnny Cash. "The Little Drummer Boy" (Columbia 41481), 1959.

George Castelle. "It's Christmas Time" (Grand 118), 1954; reissued as the Castelles (Collectibles 1056), 1990.

The Jimmy Castor Bunch. "The Christmas Song" (Atlantic 3302), 1975.

The Chambers Brothers. "Merry Christmas, Happy New Year" (Columbia 45055), 1969.

Ray Charles. "Christmas Time" (Crossover/Atlantic 3549), 1978.

Chubby Checker and Bobby Rydell. "Jingle Bell Rock" (Cameo 205), 1961.

Cheech and Chong. "Santa Claus and His Old Lady" (Ode 66021), 1971–1973; (Ode Epic 50449), 1977.

The Chipmunks. "The Chipmunk Song" (Liberty 55168), 1958; (Liberty 55250), 1959–1963; (Liberty 54583), 1968; (United Artists 065), 1973; (United Artists 056), 1973–1975; (United Artists 576), 1974; (Capitol 056), 1981.

———. "Rudolph the Red-Nosed Reindeer" (Liberty 55289), 1960–1966; (Liberty 54583), 1968; (United Artists 065), 1973; (United Artists 057) 1973–1975.

Christmas Spirit. "Christmas Is My Time of Year" (White Whale 290), 1968.

Rosemary Clooney. *See* Gene Autry and Rosemary Clooney.

King Cole Trio. "The Christmas Song" (Capitol 311), 1946; (Capitol 15201), 1948.

Nat "King" Cole. "Frosty the Snow Man" (Capitol 1203), 1950.

———. "The Christmas Song" (Capitol 90036), 1953; (Capitol 2955), 1954; (Capitol 3561), 1956.

Commander Cody. "Daddy's Drinkin' Up Our Christmas" (Dot 17487), 1972.

Perry Como. "Winter Wonderland" (RCA Victor 1968), 1946; (RCA Victor 2969), 1949.

Bill Cosby. "Merry Christmas Mama" (Capitol 4501), 1977.

Count Sidney and His Dukes. "Soul Christmas" (Goldband 1184), 1967.

The Crewcuts. "Dance Mr. Snowman Dance" (Mercury 70491), 1954.

Jim Croce. "It Doesn't Have to Be That Way" (ABC/Paramount 11413), 1973.

The Crosby Family. "A Crosby Christmas" (Decca 401081), 1950; (Decca 27249), 1950.

Bing Crosby. "Silent Night" (Decca 621), 1935.

———. "White Christmas" (Decca 18429), 1942–1945; (Decca 23778), 1946; (MCA 65022), 1973; (MCA 40830), 1977.

Bing Crosby and the Andrews Sisters. "Jingle Bells" (Decca 23281), 1943; (MCA 65019), 1973.

Bing Crosby and David Bowie. *See* David Bowie and Bing Crosby.

Bing Crosby, Danny Kaye, and Peggy Lee. "White Christmas" (Decca 29342), 1954.

Bing Crosby and Peggy Lee. "Sleigh Ride" (Decca 28463), 1952.

Bing Crosby and Frank Sinatra. "We Wish You the Merriest Christmas" (Reprise 0317), 1964.

The Crystals. "Rudolph the Red-Nosed Reindeer" (Pavillion 03333), 1982.

King Curtis. "The Christmas Song" (Atco 6630), 1968.

Vic Dana. "Little Altar Boy" (Dolton 48), 1961.

Dancer Prancer and Nervous. "The Happy Reindeer" (Capitol 4300), 1959.

Bobby Darin. "Christmas Auld Lang Syne" (Atco 6183), 1960.

The Davis Sisters. "Christmas Boogie" (RCA Victor 5906), 1954.

Doris Day. "Here Comes Santa Claus" (Columbia 38584), 1949.

Debbie and the Darnells. "Santa Teach Me How to Dance" (Vernon 101), 1962.

Delvets. "I Want a Boy for Christmas" (End 1106), 1961.

Del Vikings. "Snowbound" (Mercury 71241), 1957.

John Denver and the Muppets. "Have Yourself a Merry Little Christmas" (RCA 11767), 1979.

Jackie DeShannon. "Do You Know How Christmas Trees Are Grown" (Imperial 66403), 1969.

The Dickies. "Silent Night" (A&M 2092), 1978.

Everett McKinley Dirksen. "The First Time the Christmas Story Was Told" (Capitol 2034), 1967.

Dr. John. "Thank You Santa" (Maison De Soul 1026), 1984.

Micky Dolenz, Davy Jones, and Peter Tork. "Christmas Is My Time of Year" (Christmas 700), 1976.

Ral Donner. "(Things That Make Up) Christmas Day" (Reprise 0135), 1962; (Starfire 103), 1979.

Mike Douglas. "The First Christmas Carol" (Epic 10089), 1966.

The Drifters. "The Christmas Song" (Atlantic 2261), 1964. (*See also* Clyde McPhatter and the Drifters.)

Champion Jack Dupree. "Santa Claus Blues" (Joe Davis 5107), 1946.

Jimmy Durante. "Frosty the Snowman" (MGM 30257), 1950.

The Eagles. "Please Come Home for Christmas" (Asylum 45555), 1978; (Asylum 12" 11402), 1978.

The Ebonaires. "Love for Christmas" (Hollywood 1046), 1955.

The Echelons. "Christmas Long Ago" (Bab 129), 1987.

Billy Eckstine. "O Come All Ye Faithful" (MGM 10525), 1949.

Dave Edmunds. "Run Rudolph Run" (Columbia 03428), 1982; (Columbia 1576, 33-rpm promo), 1982.

Tommy Edwards. "Kris Kringle" (MGM 11097), 1951.

Elmo and Patsy. "Grandma Got Run Over by a Reindeer" (Kim Pat 2984), 1979. Remade (Oink 2984), 1982; reissued (Soundwaves 4658), 1982.

The Emotions. "Black Christmas" (Volt 4053), 1970.

The Enchanters. "Mambo Santa Mambo" (Coral 61916), 1957.

Dale Evans. *See* Roy Rogers and Dale Evans.

The Falcons. "Can This Be Christmas" (Silhouette 521), 1957.

Jose Feliciano. "Feliz Navidad" (RCA 0404), 1970.

Freddy Fender. "Please Come Home for Christmas" (ABC/Dot 17734), 1977.

Ella Fitzgerald. "Santa Claus Got Stuck in My Chimney" (Decca 27255), 1950.

The Five Keys. "It's Christmastime" (Aladdin 3113), 1951; (Liberty 1394), 1980.

Roberta Flack. "Twenty-fifth of Last December" (Atlantic 3441), 1977.

Dan Fogelberg. "Same Old Lang Syne" (Epic 50961), 1980.

Foghat. "Run, Run, Rudolph" (Bearsville 780), 1978.

The Four Seasons. "Santa Claus Is Coming to Town" (Vee Jay 478), 1962.

Redd Foxx. "Christmas Hard Times" (Dootone 464), 1959.

Connie Francis. "Baby's First Christmas" (MGM 13051), 1961.

Aretha Franklin. "Winter Wonderland" (Columbia 43177), 1964.

Stan Freberg. "Christmas Dragnet" (Capitol 2671), 1953; retitled "Yulnet" (Capitol 2986), 1954.

———. "Green Christma$" (Capitol 4097), 1958; (Capitol 3503), 1972.

Lowell Fulson. "Lonesome Christmas" (Swing Time 242), 1950; (Hollywood 1022), 1954.

Judy Garland. "Have Yourself a Merry Little Christmas" (Decca 23362), 1944.

David Gates. "Come Home for Christmas" (Arista 0653), 1981.

The Gems. "Love for Christmas" (Chess 1917), 1965.

Lloyd Glenn. "Sleigh Ride" (Swing Time 271), 1952.

Bobby Goldsboro. "A Christmas Wish" (United Artists 50470), 1968.

Babs Gonzales. "Be Bop Santa Claus" (King 4836), 1956; also (Brucc 122) 1956 (different recording).

———. "Rock and Roll Santa Claus" (End 1008), 1957.

Dickie Goodman. "Santa and the Touchables" (Rori 701), 1961.

Eydie Gorme. "Navidad y Año Nuevo" (Columbia 43856), 1966.

Lorne Green. "Must Be Santa" (RCA Victor 9037), 1966.

Merv Griffin. "Santa Claus Is Coming to Town a Treacher" (MGM 13638), 1966.

Lalo Guerrero. "Pancho Claus" (L&M 1000), 1956.

Bill Haley. "A Year Ago This Christmas" (Holiday 111), 1951.

Lionel Hampton. "Gin for Christmas" (Victor 26423), 1939.

The Happenings. "Have Yourself a Very Merry Christmas" (B. T. Puppy 181), 1967.

The Harmony Grits. "Santa Claus Is Coming to Town" (End 1063), 1959.

Emmylou Harris. "Light of the Stable" (Reprise 1341), 1975; (Reprise 1379), 1976; (Warner Bros. 49645), 1980.

Donny Hathaway. "This Christmas" (Atco 6799), 1970; (Atco 7066), 1976; (Atco 99956), 1982.

The Heartbeats. "After New Year's Eve" (Gee 1047), 1958.

Bobby Helms. "Jingle Bell Rock" (Decca 30513), 1957.

Jimi Hendrix. "The Little Drummer Boy" (Reprise 595), 1979; (Reprise 12" Pro A840), 1979.

The Hepsters. "Rockin' N' Rollin' with Santa Claus" (Ronel 107), 1956.

Smokey Hogg. "I Want My Baby for Christmas" (Specialty 342), 1948.

Ron Holden. "Who Says There Ain't No Santa Claus?" (Donna 1331), 1960.

The Holly Twins. "I Want Elvis for Christmas" (Liberty 55048), 1956.

John Lee Hooker. "Blues for Christmas" (Hi-Q 5018), 1960.

Lightning Hopkins. "Merry Christmas" (Decca 48306), 1953.

Johnny Horton. "They Shined Up Rudolph's Nose" (Columbia 41522), 1959.

Howdy Doody. "Howdy Doody and Santa Claus" (RCA Victor 4017), 1950.

Ferlin Husky. "Christmas Dream" (Capitol 2023), 1967.

The Ink Spots. "White Christmas" (Decca 24140), 1947.

The Insight. "Please Come Home for Christmas" (Cascade 364), 1965.

Burl Ives. "A Holly Jolly Christmas" (Decca 31695), 1964.

Mahalia Jackson. "Silent Night" (Apollo 235), 1950; (Apollo 750), 1962; (Kenwood 750), 1967.

Michael Jackson. "Up on the House Top" (Motown 1914), 1987.

Jackson Five. "Santa Claus Is Coming to Town" (Motown 1174), 1970.

Jackson Trio. "Jingle Bell Hop" (Hollywood 1046), 1955.

Sonny James. "Christmas in My Home Town" (Capitol 2958), 1954.

Jan and Dean. "Frosty the Snowman" (Liberty 55522), 1962.

Jethro Tull. "The Christmas Song" (Chrysalis 2006), 1972.

Joan Jett and the Blackhearts. "Little Drummer Boy" (Blackheart 1151), 1980; (Boardwalk 7-006), 1981; (Boardwalk 12" 5-007), 1981.

Elton John. "Step into Christmas" (MCA 65018), 1973.

Davy Jones. *See* Micky Dolenz, Davy Jones, and Peter Tork.

George Jones. "New Baby for Christmas" (Mercury 71225), 1957.

George Jones and Tammy Wynette. "Mr. and Mrs. Santa Claus" (Epic 11077), 1973.

Spike Jones. "All I Want for Christmas (Is My Two Front Teeth)" (RCA Victor 3177), 1948; (RCA Victor 4315), 1951; (RCA Victor Gold Standard 0172), 1952.

Louis Jordan. "May Every Day Be Christmas" (Decca 27806), 1951.

Danny Kaye. *See* Bing Crosby, Danny Kaye, and Peggy Lee.

Albert King. "Santa Claus Wants Some Lovin'" (Stax 0234), 1974.

B. B. King. "Christmas Celebration" (Kent 387), 1963; (Kent 412), 1964.

Earl King. "Weary, Silent Night" (Ace 564), 1959.

Freddy King. "Christmas Tears" (Federal 12439), 1961.

The Kingston Trio. "Good Night, My Baby" (Capitol 4475), 1960.

The Kinks. "Father Christmas" (Arista 0290), 1977; (Arista 12" 34), 1977.

Eartha Kitt. "Santa Baby" (RCA Victor 5502), 1953.

Gladys Knight and the Pips. "Silent Night" (Buddah 1974), 1974.

Frankie Laine. "You're All I Want for Christmas" (Mercury 5177), 1948.

Greg Lake. "I Believe in Father Christmas" (Atlantic 3305), 1975.

Clyde Lasley and His Cadillac Baby Specials. "Santa Claus Came Home Drunk" (Bea and Baby 121), 1963.

Leadbelly. "Christmas Song" (Asch 34), 1941.

Brenda Lee. "I'm Gonna Lasso Santa Claus" (Decca 88215 and 30107), 1956.

———. "Rockin' Around the Christmas Tree" (Decca 30776), 1958; (MCA 65027), 1973.

Julia Lee. "Christmas Spirits" (Capitol 15203), 1948.

Peggy Lee. *See under* Bing Crosby.

John Lennon and Yoko Ono. "Happy Xmas (War Is Over)" (Apple 1842), 1971; (Capitol 1842), 1980; (Geffen 29855), 1982.

Jerry Lee Lewis. "I Can't Have a Merry Christmas" (Mercury 73155), 1970.

The Ramsey Lewis Trio. "Winter Wonderland" (Argo 5337), 1959; (Cadet 5337), 1965.

Jimmy Liggins. "I Want My Baby for Christmas" (Specialty 380), 1950.

Ben Light and His Surf Club Boys. "Christmas Balls" (Hollywood Hot Shots 338), c. 1936, bootlegged in 1940s.

Little Cindy. "Happy Birthday, Jesus" (Columbia 41320), 1958.

Little Esther and Mel Walker. "My Christmas Blues" (Savoy 1146), 1954.

Trini Lopez. "El Niño del Tambor" (Reprise 0801), 1968.

Julie London. "I'd Like You for Christmas" (Liberty 55108), 1957.

Darlene Love. "Christmas (Baby Please Come Home)" (Philles 119), 1963; (Philles 125), 1964; (Warner Spector 0401), 1974.

Frankie Lymon. "It's Christmas Once Again" (Roulette 4035), 1957.

Loretta Lynn. "It Won't Seem Like Christmas" (Decca 32043), 1966.

Paul McCartney. "Wonderful Christmastime" (Columbia 11162), 1979.

The McGuire Sisters. "Christmas Alphabet" (Coral 61303), 1954.

Bob and Doug McKenzie. "Twelve Days of Christmas" (Mercury 76133), 1983.

Clyde McPhatter and the Drifters. "White Christmas" (Atlantic 1048), 1954. (*See also* the Drifters.)

Mad Milo. "Elvis for Christmas" (Million 20018), 1956.

The Marcels. "Merry Twist-Mas" (Colpix 617), 1961.

The Marquees. "Christmas in the Congo" (Warner Bros. 5127), 1959.

The Marshall Brothers. "Mr. Santa's Boogie" (Savoy 825), 1951.

Dean Martin. "The Christmas Blues" (Capitol 2640), 1953.

Johnny Mathis. "My Kind of Christmas" (Columbia 42238), 1961.

———. "The Little Drummer Boy" (Mercury 72217), 1963.

Nathaniel Mayer and the Fabulous Twilights. "Mr. Santa Claus" (Fortune 550), 1962.

Melanie. "Merry Christmas" (Buddah 202), 1970.

Roger Miller. "Old Toy Trains" (Smash 2130), 1967.

The Mills Brothers. "My Christmas Song for You" (Decca 24768), 1947.

Bill Monroe. "Christmas Time's a Comin'" (Decca 46386), 1952.

Montana Slim. "Jolly Old St. Nicholas" (RCA Victor 0392), 1950.

The Moonglows. "Hey Santa Claus" (Chance 1150), 1953.

Johnny Moore's Three Blazers with Charles Brown. "Merry Christmas, Baby" (Exclusive 63), 1947–1949; (Swing Time 238), 1950–1952; (Hollywood 1021), 1954.

The Phil Moore Four. "Stingy Old Scrooge" (RCA Victor 5538), 1953.

Martin Mull. "Santa Doesn't Cop Out on Dope" (Capricorn 0037), 1973.

The Muppets. *See* John Denver and the Muppets.

Willie Nelson. "Pretty Paper" (RCA Victor 8484), 1964.

The Nic Nacs and Mickey Champion. "Gonna Have a Merry Christmas" (RPM 313), 1951.

Robert Nighthawk. "Merry Christmas" (Decca 4748), 1964.

Nilsson. "Remember Christmas" (RCA 0855), 1972.

Nino and the Ebb Tides. "The Real Meaning of Christmas" (Recorte 408), 1958.

The Nitty Gritty Dirt Band. "Colorado Christmas" (Liberty 1513), 1983.

The Nutty Squirrels. "Please Don't Take Our Tree for Christmas" (Columbia 41818), 1960.

The Ohio Players. "Happy Holidays" (Mercury 73753), 1975.

The O'Jays. "Christmas Ain't Christmas, New Year's Ain't New Year's Without the One You Love" (Neptune 20), 1969; (Philadelphia International 3537), 1973.

———. "The Christmas Song" (EMI 12″ 4854), 1991.

Yoko Ono. *See* John Lennon and Yoko Ono.

Roy Orbison. "Pretty Paper" (Monument 830), 1963; (Monument 531), 1970.

The Orioles. "Lonely Christmas" (Jubilee 5001), 1948; (Jubilee 5017), 1949.

———. "What Are You Doing New Year's Eve" (Jubilee 5017), 1949; (Virgo 6017), 1972.

Jimmy Osmond. "If Santa Were My Dad" (MGM 14328), 1971.

Buck Owens and His Buckaroos. "Santa Looked a Lot Like Daddy" (Capitol 5537), 1965.

Buck Owens and Susan Raye. "Santa's Gonna Come in a Stagecoach" (Capitol 3225), 1971.

Patti Page. "Boogie Woogie Santa Claus" (Mercury 5534), 1950; (Mercury 5729), 1951.

Ray Parker, Jr. "Christmas Time Is Here" (Arista 1035), 1982.

Dolly Parton. "Hard-Candy Christmas" (RCA 13361), 1982.

Marlene Paul. "I Want to Spend Xmas with Elvis" (Regent 7506), 1956.

Paul and Paula. "Holiday Hootenanny" (Philips 40158), 1963.

Gayla Peevey. "I Want a Hippopotamus for Christmas" (Columbia 40106), 1953.

The Penguins. "A Christmas Prayer" (Mercury 70762), 1955.

Little Lambsie Penn. "I Want to Spend Christmas with Elvis" (Atco 6082), 1956.

Peter, Paul, and Mary. "A Soulin'" (Warner Bros. 5402), 1963.

Bobby "Boris" Pickett. "Monster's Holiday" (Garpax 44171), 1962; (Parrot 366), 1973.

Webb Pierce. "Christmas at Home" (Decca 31867), 1965.

The Pilgrim Travelers. "I'll Be Home for Christmas" (Specialty 837), 1952; (Specialty 934), 1959.

The Pipsqueeks. "Santa's Little Helper" (Warner Bros. 5878), 1966.

The Poets. "Merry Christmas, Baby" (Red Bird 10046), 1965.

Elvis Presley. "Blue Christmas" (RCA Victor 0808, promo), 1957; (RCA Victor Gold Standard 0720), 1964; (RCA Victor Gold Standard 0647), 1965.

———. "Merry Christmas, Baby" (RCA 0572), 1971.

Johnny Preston. "New Baby for Christmas" (Mercury 71728), 1960.

Louis Prima. "What Will Santa Claus Say?" (Vocalion 3376), 1936.

Prince. "Another Lonely Christmas" (Warner Bros. 29121), 1984.

John Prine. "I Saw Mommy Kissing Santa Claus" (Oh Boy 1), 1981.

Johnny Que. "Rockabilly Christmas" (Rhino 099), 1981.

The Ramblers. "Surfin' Santa" (Almont 315), 1964.

The Ravens. "White Christmas" (National 9062), 1948; (Mercury 70505), 1954; (Savoy 1540), 1959.

The Ravers. "(It's Gonna Be a) Punk Rock Christmas" (Zombie 7683), 1977.

Susan Raye. See Buck Owens and Susan Raye.

Otis Redding. "Merry Christmas Baby" (Atco 6631), 1968; (Atco 7069), 1976; (Atco 99955), 1982.

———. "White Christmas" (Atco 6631), 1968; (Atco 7069), 1976; (Atco 99955), 1982.

Jerry Reed. "Christmas Time's a Comin'" (RCA 13666), 1983.

The Residents. "Santa Dog" (Ralph 1272), 1972.

Bobby Rey. "Rockin' J Bells" (Original Sound 08), 1958.

Keith Richards. "Run Rudolph Run" (Rolling Stones 19311), 1978.

Augie Rios. "Donde Esta Santa Claus" (Metro 20010), 1958; (MGM 13292), 1964.

Tex Ritter. "Christmas Carols by the Old Corral" (Capitol 222), 1945; (Capitol 15204), 1948; (Capitol 1264), 1950.

Derrick Roberts. "There Won't Be Any Snow (Christmas in the Jungle)" (Roulette 4656), 1965.

The Rockin' Stockings. "Yulesville USA" (Sun 1960), 1960.

The Rocky Fellers. "Santa, Santa" (Scepter 1245), 1962.

Jimmie Rodgers. "It's Christmas Once Again" (Roulette 4205), 1959.

Kenny Rogers. "Kentucky Homemade Christmas" (Liberty 1438), 1982.

Roy Rogers. "Silent Night" (Decca 5883), 1942.

Roy Rogers and Dale Evans. "Christmas on the Plains" (RCA Victor 0125), 1949.

The Ronettes. "I Saw Mommy Kissing Santa Claus" (Pavillion 03333), 1982.

Rotary Connection. "Silent Night Chant" (Cadet Concept 7009), 1968.

Leon Russell. "Sleeping into Christmas" (Shelter 7328), 1972.

Bobby Rydell. *See* Chubby Checker and Bobby Rydell.

The Sabres. "Cool, Cool Christmas" (Cal West 847), 1955.

Staff Sgt. Barry Sadler. "I Won't Be Home for Christmas" (RCA Victor 9008), 1966.

The Salas Brothers. "Donde Esta Santa Claus" (Faro 625), 1966.

Soupy Sales. "Santa Claus Is Surfin' to Town" (Reprise 0244), 1963.

sam iam. "Santa Claus Is Dead" (Oblong 12-25), 1989.

Santo and Johnny. "Twistin' Bells" (Canadian American 120), 1960; (Canadian American 132), 1961; (Canadian American 148), 1962.

Father Guido Sarducci. "I Won't Be Twistin' This Christmas" (Warner Bros. 49627), 1980.

Jack Scott. "Jingle Bells Slide" (Groove 0027), 1963.

Linda Scott. "Christmas Day" (Canadian American 132), 1961.

Mabel Scott. "Boogie Woogie Santa Claus" (Exclusive 75), 1948.

Bob Seger and the Last Heard. "Sock It to Me Santa" (Cameo 444), 1966.

The Shells. "Happy Holiday" (Johnson 119), 1960.

Allan Sherman. "The Twelve Gifts of Christmas" (Warner Bros. 5406), 1963.

Bobby Sherman. "Goin' Home, Sing a Song of Christmas Cheer" (Metromedia 204), 1970.

The Harry Simeone Chorale. "The Little Drummer Boy" (20th Fox 121), 1958–1962; (20th Fox 429), 1963–1966; (20th Fox 6429), 1967; (Mistletoe/Trip 800), 1976.

Frank Sinatra. "White Christmas" (Columbia 36756), 1944; (Columbia 36860), 1945; (Columbia 37152), 1946; (Columbia 38257), 1948.

———. "Have Yourself a Merry Little Christmas" (Reprise 0243), 1963.

Frank Sinatra and Bing Crosby. *See* Bing Crosby and Frank Sinatra.

Nancy Sinatra. "Such a Lonely Time of Year" (Reprise 0880), 1969.

The Sinatra Family. "Whatever Happened to Christmas" (Reprise 0790), 1968.

The Singing Dogs. "Jingle Bells" (RCA Victor 6344), 1955; (RCA 1020), 1971; (RCA 10127), 1983.

The Skyliners. "You're My Christmas Present" (Classic Artists 123), 1990.

Hank Snow. "Reindeer Boogie" (RCA Victor 5340), 1953.

The Sonics. "Don't Believe in Christmas" (Etiquette 22), 1965.

The Soul Stirrers. "Christmas Joy" (Chess 5007), 1966.

Bruce Springsteen. "Santa Claus Is Coming to Town" (Columbia 05728), 1985.

———. "Merry Christmas Baby" (Columbia 06432), 1986.

Billy Squier. "Christmas Is the Time to Say I Love You" (Capitol 5037), 1981; (Capitol 5303), 1983.

The Staple Singers. "Who Took the Merry out of Christmas" (Stax 0844), 1970.

Star Wars Intergalactic Droid Choir. "What Can You Get a Wookie for Christmas" (RSO 1058), 1980.

The Statues. "White Christmas" (Liberty 55292), 1960.

Dodie Stevens. "Merry Merry Christmas Baby" (Dot 16166), 1960.

Ray Stevens. "Santa Claus Is Watching You" (Mercury 72058), 1962.

The Supremes. "Twinkle Twinkle Little Me" (Motown 1085), 1965.

The Surfaris. "The Surfer's Christmas List" (Decca 31561), 1963.

Little Johnny Taylor. "Please Come Home for Christmas" (Galaxy 743), 1965.

The Temptations. "Silent Night" (Gordy 7082), 1968.

Joe Tex. "I'll Make Everyday Christmas" (Dial 4068), 1967.

Sister Rosetta Tharpe. "Silent Night" (Decca 48119), 1949; (Decca 25760), 1969.

Carla Thomas. "Gee Whiz, It's Christmas" (Atlantic 2212), 1963; (Stax 206), 1966.

Hank Thompson. "I'd Like to Have an Elephant for Christmas" (Capitol 5310), 1964.

George Thorogood. "Rock and Roll Christmas" (EMI-America 8187), 1983.

Johnny Tillotson. "Christmas Country Style" (MGM 13633), 1966.

Timbuk 3. "All I Want for Christmas" (I.R.S. 53221), 1987.

Peter Tork. *See* Micky Dolenz, Davy Jones, and Peter Tork.

The Trashmen. "Dancing with Santa" (Garrett 4013), 1964.

The Travelers. "I'll Be Home for Christmas" (Andex 2011), 1958.

Ernest Tubb. "Blue Christmas" (Decca 46186), 1949; (Decca 25758), 1969; (MCA 65024), 1973.

The Tune Weavers. "Merry, Merry Christmas, Baby" (Classic Artists 107), 1988.

Ike and Tina Turner. "Merry Christmas, Baby" (Warner Bros. 5493), 1964.

Joe Turner. "Christmas Date Boogie" (Down Beat 153), 1948.

The Uniques. "Merry Christmas, Darling" (Demand 2936; Dot 16533), 1963.

U2. "New Year's Day" (Island 99915), 1983.

The Valentines. "Christmas Prayer" (Rama 186), 1955.

The Ventures. "Sleigh Ride" (Dolton 312), 1965.

The Voices. "Santa Claus Baby," "Santa Claus Boogie" (Cash 1016), 1955.

The Wailers. "Christmas Spirit" (Etiquette 22), 1965.

Jimmy Wakely. "Christmas on the Range" (Capitol 90015), 1948.

Mel Walker. *See* Little Esther and Mel Walker.

Fats Waller. "Swingin' the Jingle Bells" (Victor 25490), 1936; (Victor 1602), 1944; (RCA Victor 1602), 1946.

Billy Ward and the Dominoes. "Christmas in Heaven" (King 1281), 1953.

Joe Ward. "Nuttin' for Christmas" (King 4854), 1955.

Fred Waring and His Pennsylvanians. " 'Twas the Night Before Christmas" (Decca 18499), 1942; (Decca 23642), 1946.

Dinah Washington. "Silent Night" (Mercury 70263), 1953.

The Weather Girls. "Dear Santa" (Columbia 04299), 1983.

The Weavers. "We Wish You a Merry Christmas" (Decca 27783), 1951.

West Coast. "Christmas Time" (Dee Jay 201), 1987.

The Whispers. "Happy Holidays to You" (Solar 11449), 1978.

Andy Williams. "Christmas Is a Feeling in Your Heart" (Cadence 1282), 1955.

———. "Do You Hear What I Hear?" (Columbia 43458), 1965.

Clarence Williams. "Christmas Night in Harlem" (Vocalion 2689), 1934.

Sonny Boy Williamson. "Sonny Boy's Christmas Blues" (Trumpet 145), 1953.

Willis "the Guard" and Vigorish. "Merry Christmas in the NFL" (Handshake 5300), 1980.

Bob Wills and His Texas Playboys. "Empty Chairs at the Christmas Table" (Columbia 36881), 1945; (Columbia 20008), 1947.

Jackie Wilson. "O Holy Night" (Brunswick 55254), 1963.

Tony Wine. "My Boyfriend's Coming Home for Christmas" (Colpix 715), 1963.

Stevie Wonder. "Someday at Christmas" (Tamla 54142), 1966.

Roy Wood's Wizzards. "I Wish It Could be Christmas Everyday" (United Artists 1103), 1977.

Sheb Wooley. "Here Comes Santa Claus" (MGM 12733), 1958.

Tammy Wynette. "One Happy Christmas" (Epic 10690), 1970. (*See also* George Jones and Tammy Wynette.)

Weird Al Yankovic. "Christmas at Ground Zero" (Rock 'n' Roll 06588), 1986.

Dwight Yoakam. "Santa Claus Is Back in Town" (Reprise 7-28156), 1987.

Yogi Yorgesson. "Yingle Bells" (Capitol 781), 1949; (Capitol 2904), 1957.

Faron Young. "You're the Angel in My Christmas Tree" (Capitol 2629), 1953.

The Youngsters. "Christmas in Jail" (Empire 109), 1956.

ᴀcknowledgments

James Austin, Harold Bronson, Charles Brown, Sandra Choron, Nate Cohen, Tony D'Amico, Jim Dawson, Barry Hansen, Fred Hoyt, Wayne Kline, Malcolm Leo, Neil McCormick, Larry Orr, Ray Peavy, Michael Pietsch, Ken Poston, and Mike Stark.

Merry Christmas to all, and to all a good night.